Especially for

_____

From

_____

Date

_____

THE
MAN
MINUTE

THE
MAN
MINUTE

60 Seconds Can Change Your Life. . .

JASON
CRUISE

BARBOUR BOOKS
An Imprint of Barbour Publishing, Inc.

© 2015 by Jason Cruise

Print ISBN 978-1-68322-414-3

eBook Editions:
Adobe Digital Edition (.epub) 978-1-63409-408-5
Kindle and MobiPocket Edition (.prc) 978-1-63409-409-2

Published by Barbour Books, an imprint of Barbour Publishing, Inc., 1810 Barbour Drive, Uhrichsville, Ohio 44683, www.barbourbooks.com

Our mission is to inspire the world with the life-changing message of the Bible.

Member of the
Evangelical Christian
Publishers Association

Printed in the United States of America.

PREFACE

Who knows why this book ended up in your hands? Perhaps you received it as a Christmas gift, or maybe your kids picked one up for you in hopes of filling the gap on Father's Day. Many things in life seem random.

There's often something unexpected about the way God moves a man forward; at least that's my experience. I've noticed that more often than not, God moves a man forward quietly. It's odd, really. No lightning split the sky the day I came to Christ, and no thunder shook the kitchen floor the day I first thought of putting out a word of truth that a man could read in about 60 seconds. These things happened on seemingly ordinary days.

With 60 seconds in mind, I didn't put much thought into it when I gave the original series the title of *The Man Minute*. It seemed to fit decently enough, I suppose.

Very quietly thereafter, God took His normal approach of moving something forward in men. To be completely candid, I cannot explain it. I cannot explain why other projects I've launched didn't move very far, and something as seemingly random as *The Man Minute* has spanned denominations, people groups, and even oceans to get inside the souls of men of all walks of life.

I cannot attempt to explain why *The Man Minute* fell into your world, either, but it has no doubt landed on the path of your journey. I cannot tell you what's going to happen to you as you encounter scripture throughout this journey, other than to say that your life won't be the same. You're going to have God say things to you through some of these 60-second time investments—and only He will know the reasons the words hit you the way they did.

God doesn't take part in the coincidental, and He doesn't offer random. His paths are sure and battle tested. And His words are worth slowing down long enough to encounter.

Now that our paths have crossed, my heartbeat for you is that you never rush the 60 seconds as you read *The Man Minute*, because I know from experience that God can do a lot to a man in just a minute.

Now to him who is able to do immeasurably more than all we ask or imagine, according to his power that is at work within us, to him be glory in the church and in Christ Jesus throughout all generations, for ever and ever! Amen.
Ephesians 3:20–21

YOU'LL FIND IT
(IF YOU REALLY WANT IT)

*The Pharisees and the teachers of the law were looking
for a reason to accuse Jesus, so they watched him
closely to see if he would heal on the Sabbath.*
LUKE 6:7

If you want to see the beauty of life, you'll find ways to make
it happen. The opposite is true as well. If you want to find
fault in people, it's easy to do, and it won't take you long to
accomplish your mission.

I know I have junk going on inside my bones. In fact,
you'd be better off just coming to me and letting me tell you
where my weaknesses reside. Believe me, I know where they
live.

Religious leaders followed Jesus around town—not with
open hearts, but rather to find any reason whatsoever to
bring Him down. Jesus was without sin, but that didn't stop
them. In the absence of sin, people will often create trouble
for you—even if you are the Sinless One sent to redeem all
humanity.

These mockers had seen Jesus' miracles, had seen love
in action. That's not enough, though, when you're a religious
snob. They had to find fault, or else they would have to look
into the mirror.

Let us never be like those religious leaders. Let us never
be the kind of people who go out of our way to find fault in
others.

WHAT NOT TO DO

---

*Like one who takes away a garment on a
cold day, or like vinegar poured on a wound,
is one who sings songs to a heavy heart.*
PROVERBS 25:20

Having spent more than twenty years in ministry, I've learned that when people's dreams are crushed or their hearts are breaking, the worst thing you can do is to play the part of the cavalier pied piper with an upbeat song. It's cold to sing songs to a troubled heart.

Don't misunderstand: the scriptures are not telling you to withhold songs of hope. People depend on hope, for the absence of hope can cause someone to follow harmful paths. Be sure to offer hope, but be careful how you package it. When people are heartbroken, the last thing they need is the guilt that comes from hearing someone say, "It's all good. Just praise the Lord anyway."

I've learned that deep despair causes people to ask questions, and those questions—when pain is too fresh for praise—tend to drown out songs of joy. What people remember most in times of heartache is that you were there. The best way you can help them is through the glorious simplicity of your presence, because that reminds them that God hasn't left them stranded.

NEGLECT

*"Who am I, Sovereign LORD, and what is my family,
that you have brought me this far?"*

2 SAMUEL 7:18

I recently felt the strong pressing of God's hand on my heart
concerning neglect—specifically my neglect of Him. I had
been letting anything and everything move in line ahead of
Him, and I had been neglecting taking the time to have consistent conversations with the God who made me.

King David said something that will forever haunt me.
God is moving among His people, and the ark of the covenant is on the move as well. David begins to have visions
of building God a proper house. God shares His vision for
His people through Nathan the prophet, and David is over-
whelmed that he's a part of the plan.

It's then that David asks, "Who am I?"—a question that
shows the king's astonishment that God would desire a man
like him. It's a question I ask myself often.

We live in a world of upside-down wisdom, and it's easy
to think that something is so important that it gets priority
over daily conversations with God. Too often I bow to that
way of thinking.

I know God doesn't *need* me to talk with Him. He's not
in need of anything. But for some reason, He's made me a part
of His plan. Because of His wonderful, unexplainable love for
me, He *wants* me to talk with Him, because He knows my
very life depends on it.

I just can't afford to neglect the time He wants to spend
with me.

WHAT YOU CAN BECOME

Judas son of James, and Judas Iscariot,
who became a traitor.
LUKE 6:16

The Gospel of Luke refers to Judas as the man who "became" a traitor. Things like that can happen to a man when he gives over his heart to his own whims.

No man in his right mind just gets up one day and says to himself, "I'm going to have sex with a woman who isn't my wife." No man gets up in the morning thinking, *I think I'd like to embezzle money from my company and spend the next few years in prison.*

I'm sure if you walked up to Judas just twelve months before he betrayed Jesus and told him he would sell Jesus' whereabouts to those looking to arrest Him, he would have looked at you as though you were sent straight from the devil.

Every time I've asked someone who's had a great failure in his past about how it happened, there is always one common denominator: it didn't happen overnight. Every one of these men can point back to a specific time when things started to slip.

A man usually doesn't just *fall* into serious sin. Rather, it's often a slow descent culminating in the terrible realization that he's become something he never dreamed he could be.

OUT OF OPTIONS

But when she could hide him no longer, she got a
papyrus basket for him and coated it with tar and pitch.
Then she placed the child in it and put it among
the reeds along the bank of the Nile.
EXODUS 2:3

I never knew pain—real soul pain—until I became a father. There is something about watching your kids go through pain that takes you to places your own personal pain simply cannot take you.

Imagine the torment Moses' mother went through as she placed her infant child in a homemade floatable basket and released him to the river. That's desperation beyond comprehension, and it required tremendous trust in God. It was either that or have him killed—for that was the edict passed down from Pharaoh, that any Hebrew who gave birth to a boy must turn him over to be thrown into the river to drown.

Sometimes I wonder how we as the people of God treat a world that doesn't know Him at all. I wonder how we affect a doubting world when we so casually throw around the idea of "trusting God with everything."

As Jesus followers, we often reduce trusting God to a message of, "Hey, if you were a better person, a stronger person, a true believer, then you'd just trust God. It's that simple."

Okay, fine. Then go ahead and put your eight-week-old son on a homemade float and send him down the nearest river. How simple is it to trust God then?

When you encounter people who are in unthinkable situations, always tell them the truth. Tell them that trusting God is their best option. Testify to that truth, but by all means testify gently. What a person whose world is collapsing needs in that moment isn't a flippant theologian but a real friend who speaks the truth in gentleness and love.

WHAT YOU THINK YOU NEED

"Which is easier: to say, 'Your sins are forgiven,' or to say, 'Get up and walk'? But I want you to know that the Son of Man has authority on earth to forgive sins." So he said to the paralyzed man, "I tell you, get up, take your mat and go home." Immediately he stood up in front of them, took what he had been lying on and went home praising God.
LUKE 5:23–25

I think Jesus intended all along to heal the paralyzed man whose friends had brought him to Him for healing. I think He saw an opportunity to address some toxic chemicals buried within the hearts of the religious elite at the scene, and He wasn't going to miss it.

Jesus showed everyone in that crowd that there are things you think you need, and then there are things beyond that, things God knows you really need.

This man probably thought his greatest need in life was to walk again—and who could blame him? If I couldn't walk, I'm sure walking would consume my thoughts every day.

However, even if this man's legs worked perfectly, sin would still paralyze his soul. Healthy legs would have simply allowed him to walk into hell on his own instead of being carried there by others.

What he needed most was not the ability to walk, but a free soul. And Jesus was more than willing to offend some religious elites to teach us that lesson.

RECKLESS PEOPLE

*Better to meet a bear robbed of
her cubs than a fool bent on folly.*
PROVERBS 17:12

Can you imagine hiking through the woods and encountering a grizzly sow who cannot locate her cubs? The truth is, there is most likely less than a 1 percent chance you'd walk away from that encounter without suffering severe bodily harm, most likely death, at the paws of a beast that can kill not only quickly, but without remorse. You'd call any man a fool's fool to mess with a panic-stricken sow. In fact, most of us would readily admit that such a man got what was coming to him.

So put the thought of that kind of encounter into the context of Solomon's wisdom about people who live recklessly. A "fool bent on folly" is a man who has abandoned common sense and caring. He is bent, meaning the hardwiring of his soul no longer craves that which is in alignment with the heart of God.

I've watched men become reckless. It's an ugly thing. Too many times I've heard men relay to me that they honestly believed they were immune to the depravity of those within their circle. That same thinking is akin to thinking you can encounter the panicked sow and walk away unscathed.

The wisdom behind Solomon's words is this: stay away from those who live recklessly, for if you put yourself within their circle, you will not escape without scars. Reckless people wreck people. Whether or not you think it's possible, they will take you with them to places you don't want to go.

WHICH FATHER TO LISTEN TO

*My son, keep your father's command and do not forsake
your mother's teaching. Bind them always on your heart;
fasten them around your neck. When you walk, they will
guide you; when you sleep, they will watch over you;
when you awake, they will speak to you.*

PROVERBS 6:20-22

Solomon wrote of the wisdom of listening to your father and mother. But it has occurred to me that his core message is directed at those who follow Yahweh.

The apostle Paul called our enemy, Satan, the "father of lies." And if a man is not in Christ, then he will listen to and follow that father, the one who wants to sway his spirit away from his heavenly Father. The devil often disguises himself as one speaking with a voice of reason, and he often tells men to "follow what you think is best."

Whose voice do you listen to—that of the heavenly Father, who always has your best interests in mind, or that of the father of lies, who wants you to do only what you want to do? If you are in Christ, then a new spirit is in you, and you can trust your heart to hear the voice of your heavenly Father. You are not obliged to follow what you hear or feel in the moment. Rather, you can "bind" the teachings of your Father on your heart so that "they will guide you."

START WITH WHERE
YOU'RE STANDING NOW

"You have been faithful with a few things;
I will put you in charge of many things."
MATTHEW 25:21

Envy can reveal itself in subtle forms. Envy, like every other sin, is often the starting place leading in a direction far away from God. Because sin usually starts small, you tend not to notice it so much—and something as subtle as envy feels a long way from stealing or murder.

So often when I speak at men's events, I hear men talk about how they wish they could have a place in ministry that impacts men. The truth is, they do have that place, but they don't recognize it.

A man will often look at what he wishes he had instead of looking at what he actually has in front of him. This is Satan's way of keeping him on the bench, entertaining thoughts of getting into the game.

My grandfather fought in World War II, and he was once assigned to a unit that, in his words, "had a lot of city boys in it." He recalled a time when the men were starving because it had been days since they'd even seen any real food. Then they pushed through some timber and entered a field in the German countryside. My grandfather's heart exhaled with relief, but one of the men lamented, "When are we ever going to find some food?" My grandfather answered, "Boys, we're standing on potatoes."

Cultivate the field you're standing in right at this moment. It's the only field God has given you for now, and He wants you to work it as hard as you can. Read between the lines of Jesus' story of faithfulness, and you'll find this important truth: God won't give you larger fields to work until you plow the ground you're standing on today.

SMALL THINGS

*Every good and perfect gift is from above,
coming down from the Father of the heavenly lights,
who does not change like shifting shadows.*
JAMES 1:17

Not long ago I was on a personal retreat—planning, praying, and just spending personal time with God. I figured that if I went to Bozeman, Montana, I'd be in the mountains—literally closer to God—and thus my spiritual reception would be stronger.

I remember getting up one morning, sitting on the steps of the cabin and enjoying the view of the mountains, and praying something like this: "God, don't let me miss You in the small things today." I had no idea what that prayer was about to do to me, in me, and around me. I soon found out.

It started with the owner of River's Edge Fly Shop spending an incredible amount of time with me, showing me some of his hot spots on the local rivers. It continued as a girl at a coffee shop—who seemed to be energized by helping others, even someone buying a single cup of coffee—treated me like a true friend.

After spending some time planning and looking into my ministry work, I was on my way to get dinner at a local diner in Bozeman. It was then that I hit a time warp that has messed with my brain to this day. I had run out of gas just once, and that was in high school. Once was enough, for I learned that living on the edge of a low tank wasn't worth the hassle. My own vehicle is a Toyota Tundra, and when its low fuel warning light comes on, I know I have about forty miles left. That wasn't the case with the truck I'd rented. Apparently, when the gas light came on in that vehicle, it was its way of saying, "Life is about to get painful for you if you don't find a gas station in forty-seven seconds."

Within ten minutes of running out of fuel, I was in a car headed to a gas station. It was driven by a husband and wife—the Reids—who treated me as if I were their grandson in need of assistance as they helped me get back on the road.

When I finally got to a local restaurant, I found it was going to close in about thirty minutes. My food came fairly fast, but I basically had the place to myself. Ross, one of the attendants, approached me and asked, "What kind of music do you like?"

For some reason, at that moment I chose to say, "Classic country." He immediately changed the background music to classic country, and out came Waylon over the speakers. "You didn't have to do that," I said.

"Well, why not?" he answered, and we entered into a long conversation about how rare it is to see businesses do the small things for people nowadays.

I felt the encouragement of God surrounding me so thick that I could almost breathe it in, and just then I remembered that I had asked God to keep me from missing Him in the small things that day.

I couldn't help but wonder how many days I'd had just like this one, when so many things went my way, yet I simply couldn't see it. . .because I wasn't looking.

CHOKED BY OTHER PURSUITS

*"The seed that fell among thorns stands for those who hear,
but as they go on their way they are choked by life's worries,
riches and pleasures, and they do not mature."*
LUKE 8:14

At its core, worry is the fear of not getting what you think you're going to need in a given situation. When we worry about the acquisition of something we think we need, it is actually because we worry that we won't have the security or significance we think we need.

I believe the parable of the sower is about people who actually receive the Word of God but end up placing other pursuits higher in value. This story is a warning that when we rank listening to God low on our list of priorities, then other "voices" will choke out His voice altogether.

Men want something worth living for, and when the heart chooses something other than living for God and His kingdom, true life, life sprung from living water, is dammed up and choked out.

I believe this is why Jesus used the idea of maturity in this parable. People who choose the pleasures of this world as their reason for living base their life motive on immaturities of the soul. Therefore, God's Word—His truth—dwindles in the presence of their hectic pursuits.

In reality, what we see here is Idolatry 101. It's not that God or His Word has a weak footing in competing values for the heart; it's simply that He will let you have your way. And if you find your "pleasure" in other gods, then don't be shocked when the voice of the true God is silent in your life.

DRAINED

Do not spend your strength on women,
your vigor on those who ruin kings.
PROVERBS 31:3

A man who chases the fantasy of other women will find that the sex might be exhilarating for a while but the long-term damage will far outweigh the allure of the taboo. Sadly, most men who have allowed this fantasy to become reality never stopped to consider the consequences. And when the glitter and thrill of the fantasy wore off, all they had left was a new set of problems with a bigger set of teeth.

Ask nearly anyone who has been involved in an affair, and they will tell you that it drained them in the end. The added drama, the damage done to relationships with friends and family, the destruction of reputation, and the chaos that ensues after everything is exposed to the public. . .all these things are proof that sexual sin brings with it heavy and lasting consequences.

The short-term gain of an affair is never profitable—it will always lead to loss.

SIN WAS NO SHOCKER

*"Why do you eat and drink with
tax collectors and sinners?"*
Luke 5:30

When the religious leaders during Jesus' time on earth asked Him why He dined with sinners, their question provided a window into their own spiritual condition, for what they were really saying was, "These miserable sinners are beneath us."

The religious elites constantly hammered Jesus for spending so much of His time with sinners. There is some unintentional humor in these criticisms. First of all, they didn't understand that Jesus had come to earth to spend time with sinners and show them the way to God. Second, like us today, Jesus couldn't have avoided sinners even if He had wanted to. Everywhere He went, there were sinners. Every person He met was a sinner, and every conversation He engaged in was with a sinner—even if the sinner didn't know it.

Jesus wasn't threatened by sin. He never excused it; in fact, He came to earth to die and come out of the grave to redeem people from it. But He understood the simple truth that every person born into this world carries the spiritual baggage of sin.

Sadly, it was the "churchgoin' folk" of Jesus' day who seemed most threatened by sin. And if we today allow ourselves to be like them, then there's no way we'll be able to show a lost and hurting world the way to God through Jesus Christ.

WHEN YOU DON'T DIE

"Then they will go away to eternal punishment,
but the righteous to eternal life."
MATTHEW 25:46

Perhaps the greatest lie Satan has perpetrated on the human race today is this gem: "You only live once." That may be a great slogan for a bumper sticker, but, to employ a Southernism, "it just ain't true."

God has made it expressly clear that every man lives forever. The issue isn't whether he lives forever, but where he'll be living when forever starts.

Let's get personal about this: If you really believe you're going to live forever, then how has that belief affected you in the here and now? How does it affect the way you live or the way you view the world around you?

There are likely dozens of ways to answer that question, but what stays at the forefront of my mind is this: since I'm going to live forever, how I live here on earth and what I leave behind me matters a lot, because my life's work will live beyond me—here on earth, anyway.

SOMETHING I NEVER ASK GOD

In the journey that is my relationship with God, I have asked Him for many things. There's nothing I won't talk with Him about, but it has occurred to me that I need to ask Him for something I didn't think I needed to ask for, something I thought I already had inside me.

Let me explain.

I sit on the board of Justice and Mercy International, an amazing organization that combats human trafficking and injustice perpetrated on children in Moldova and Brazil. At the opening of one of our recent meetings, one of our board members prayed and asked God that we would have faith—that our faith would increase in who He is as our God and our leader.

At that moment, it struck me that I couldn't remember ever specifically asking God to deepen my faith in Him. I had been saved by faith and I had faith in who God is in me and in what He can do in any given situation. However, I don't think I'd ever looked at faith as a well that can be dug deeper so that it can take in more water.

I want within me a faith that knows no limits. I understand that faith is supernatural, and I understand that possessing that kind of faith means I need a supernatural work done inside me.

For that to happen, I'm going to have to ask God to do the work.

FINANCIAL SECURITY

*Someone in the crowd said to [Jesus], "Teacher,
tell my brother to divide the inheritance with me."*
LUKE 12:13

Financial security is a concern of every man. Some men are better than others at overcoming the fear of not having enough money, but no man is completely immune to worrying about this issue.

After hearing Jesus go deep about fearing the God who has eternal power over our souls, a man makes a truly pathetic request: "Tell my brother to divide the inheritance with me." It's almost as if he views Jesus, the Son of God standing before him, as some sort of community leader whose job it is to make sure his brother releases the funds he thinks he needs to feel financially secure.

Before you laugh at the guy, take a look at yourself. It's likely that money and the false sense of security it brings have a deeper hold on you than you realize.

Money is immediate. Bank statements show no mercy, for they do not lie. They command respect, and they can inject peace into your soul or steal that peace from you in a matter of seconds.

Later on in this chapter, Jesus uses a phrase that stands out to me: "rich toward God" (Luke 12:21). But what exactly does that mean?

I don't fully understand what it means to be "rich toward God," but I believe it starts with this understanding: if I look at financial security as something I can lock down—making me secure no matter what—then I'll allow myself to go down a path feeding a stray dog with an appetite that demands food at every step.

WHEN SOMEONE YOU KNOW DOUBTS GOD

Be merciful to those who doubt.
JUDE 1:22

Too often we treat those who doubt the validity of the message of salvation through Jesus Christ as if they are permanently locked in rebellion. Yes, those who don't acknowledge Jesus as their Savior are in rebellion, but they don't understand rebellion as we understand it. I believe that is one of the reasons God tells us to "be merciful to those who doubt."

We're often quick to judge, aren't we? We treat doubters' or skeptics' questions with quick rebuttals or snarky religious comebacks, or we just dismiss them as people who simply want to snub God.

When we talk to doubters about our relationship with God, we often make the mistake of expecting our words to take effect immediately. I think we do this because we have forgotten what it was like to live on the other side of the cross.

Having mercy on someone who doubts God—and whose life reflects that doubt—doesn't mean excusing his lifestyle. We must be honest with doubters about a life lived in resistance to God, for honesty is the only thing that can put them in position to allow God to shape their eternal future.

Mercy means treating those who doubt God as eternal beings who are of great worth to God. It means listening to their questions without answering in ways that make them feel spiritually inferior. It may also mean remembering that there was a time when church people looked at us the way we look at them now.

Jude knew a lot about mercy. After all, his brother, Jesus Christ, was a master at it.

THINK LIKE A KING

"Or suppose a king is about to go to war against another king. Won't he first sit down and consider whether he is able with ten thousand men to oppose the one coming against him with twenty thousand?"

Luke 14:31

Many of the kings whose stories are etched in the scriptures were (most of the time anyway) men of intense wisdom. After all, a man doesn't usually become a king without a hefty dose of talent and the smarts it takes to navigate the social landscape and come out ahead.

When Jesus talked about kings in Luke 14:31, He was making this point about the nature of discipleship: if you want to follow the man from Nazareth, then you'd better know what you're in for. Counting the cost of following Christ means having wisdom to do it right.

A disciple of Christ demonstrates strength, not weakness, when he surveys his situation and demonstrates the wisdom it takes to know which battles he can win and which battles are best to avoid.

The older I get, the more I realize that wisdom, *God-honoring* wisdom, is found in knowing when to go to war and when to negotiate. It's not that I'm unwilling to fight—I just know that even if I win, I'm likely to come away bruised. . .or worse.

When you face a situation that makes you want to draw up battle plans, ask yourself, "Would a handshake work better?"

WHAT I HATE MOST

During this past turkey season, I spent some time hunting with a man who, over the years, has become a source of unmatched wisdom to me. Steve Chapman is a nationally known singer/songwriter, with equal acclaim as an author. Steve squeezed the trigger on a strutter, and we watched yet another bird fall victim to his old Mossberg 835.

On the way home, Steve pulled a package out of his truck. It was a CD entitled *Revival*, and this time Steve wasn't on the cover. It was his son, Nathan Chapman.

Nathan is a legendary music producer in Nashville. No kidding. I could rattle off the celebrities and number-one records Nate has produced, but he wouldn't like that. . .so I won't do it. Humility is a cherished component of the Chapman tribe, and thus I'll yield.

There was, however, one track I simply couldn't stop playing.

When I listened to it the first time, I cried. Out of nowhere, I found tears in my eyes. I cried because it made me think of a question a man recently asked me: "What do you see that breaks your heart the most?"

In the track "I Broke the World," the voice from Nathan's pen states, "Well what do I tell her, and you know she will ask me, 'Why don't we live in the same house as Daddy?' And you know how it hurts, when she starts to cry, because you know there's no answer to the question, 'Why?' I didn't break your heart, I broke the world."

When my friend asked me, "What gets to you the most?" I said without hesitation, "Divorce."

His look was one of astonishment. I know the look. I know it well. When most people ask this question, they think I'm going to say drug addiction or rape or the death of a child. They expect my response will speak to something truly tragic and ugly and lingering. What most people don't know is that I can think of nothing I've seen that is more tragic and ugly and lingering than divorce.

This is hard for me to talk about with you, my brothers, because I know many of you have lived the ugly, lingering tragedy. For some of you, divorce chose you; you didn't choose it.

I know you hurt over it. Which is why we must talk about it, because divorce is awful. When God says in Malachi 2:16, "I hate divorce...," He means it.

Our heavenly Father knows that divorce rips apart lives. It impacts children, who become adults, who then have to pay to see therapists because they can't pinpoint why they are so angry...until the therapist helps them trace it back to the devastation of watching their mom and dad rip up the root system of their home.

There likely are some of you reading this right now who have recently talked to a lawyer about your options. The pain in your heart is screaming just as loud as your last argument. It's the same broken record that won't stop playing, fight after fight. The silence in your marriage is deafening, and no matter how many drinks you have, you know it simply isn't going to get any better...so you're looking at pulling up roots.

Brother, this is what I know: there is no marriage so broken that God cannot make it beautiful again. Redemption is His specialty. Redemption is not without payment, however. The cost is that you must be willing to be redeemed.

SOMETHING EVERY
CHRISTIAN CAN DO

I believe that being a pastor of a local church is one of the top five toughest careers a person can pursue. The reason I believe this so strongly comes down to a simple principle: everyone who attends church has their own definition of what it means to be a "good" pastor.

Think about it. . .every person who goes to your church has their very own personalized and polished concept of what a pastor should and should not do to be effective in his job. And therein lies the problem: every person measures their pastor by their own definition.

When I pastored churches, if I spent ten hours a week visiting nursing homes, my senior citizen church members thought I was the godliest, most compassionate man they could ever ask for in a pastor. If I spent a lot of time investing in businessmen, my corporate leaders thought I was on the cutting edge of marketplace ministry. You can see where this is going. Everyone who has ever called me "Pastor" has measured *my* calling by *their* definition.

This is why I believe a great number of pastors are stricken with internalized anger, frustration, burnout, and cynicism. No, you'll likely never see it. . .or at least you won't see it until the bitter end arrives—when he's ready to resign and walk away.

Is every pastor angry, frustrated, burned out and cynical? No, of course not; but every pastor faces this discouraging cycle quite often throughout his career, and there is something you can do about it. Yes, there is something *you can do*, and you can start today.

Encourage your pastor, because I can promise you, you do not actually encourage him as much as you think you do. Your encouragement lives in your mind, but it rarely finds its way to your mouth. It's human nature, and we all make the brutal mistake of loving someone in our minds but failing to love them with our words. Speak life into your pastor's bones. Speak it often.

Give him permission to be the man God has called him to be without projecting onto his life *your* definition of what *his* calling should be. Yes, you have leadership concepts that you believe are central to ministry, and that's good. However, your pastor is not going to fit precisely into your job description. Can you imagine having forty-seven (or more!) different job descriptions? That's manic, and yet it's what a pastor deals with daily. So be easy on him.

You can be easy on your pastor. You can be the one person where, when his phone rings and he sees your name, he doesn't think, *Good grief. What now?*

I arrived home last night from leading a pastors' conference. I was reminded yet again of the load my brothers carry. I can promise you, your pastor is a good man. Yes, he's imperfect; yet in all of his imperfections, he's doing what he feels is best to lead you and your people toward a meaningful walk with God.

Be easy on your pastor.

NOT AN ORPHAN

God's views on orphans never meant as much to me as they did when I first went to Moldova with Justice and Mercy International and actually looked into the eyes of children who had no home or parents. And His feelings about injustice never completely registered in my heart until I held a young girl as she cried because she felt trapped in a world she couldn't see any hope of escaping.

I cannot imagine being an orphan, yet now I know many, many orphans. I know their names, and I have some insight into their struggles. So when Jesus says to me, "I will not leave you as orphans" (John 14:18), it carries a deeper meaning now that I've met those who wonder if anyone knows they are alive.

Not being left an orphan redefines who I am as I navigate this earthly battle for manhood and meaning. I know I don't need to worry about the security of my future, for my heavenly Father has told me what's to come. I don't need to lie awake at night fighting sleep out of fear of what may happen to me if I don't wake up, for I know the exact location of my permanent residence.

I'm not without a family name. I know exactly who my Father is, and I bear His name.

I'm not without an identity or a purpose, for I have a Father who has called me His son and an heir to His throne.

God has made good on His promise. I am not an orphan left alone to fight my way through this world.

SHEDDING

Christ in you, the hope of glory.
COLOSSIANS 1:27

Think about your most prized possession—that one material thing you'd want to hold on to if you lost everything else. That prized possession would be different for all of us. To be honest, I'm not even sure what that possession would be.

A whitetail buck doesn't have the option of holding on to his most prized possession. Every single year he loses the single most defining feature that makes him who he is: his antlers.

I've hunted some amazing places. I'll never forget the day I encountered the largest whitetail I've ever seen. We were filming a project at Tecomate Ranch in Texas. Thirty minutes into the first hunt, a buck stepped into the *sendero* we were overlooking. He was a perfect 185-inch 10-pointer with a 29-inch spread. He looked like a mule deer—a *big* mule deer.

If you can read between the lines—or perhaps I should say, if you can look past the antlers—then you know there's some deception going on here. Yes, that deer was a trophy. . . a trophy among trophies, in fact. His antlers were not what made him a trophy. What really made him a trophy was what was going on inside of him. Inside him, there were blood vessels, proteins, guanines, and other stuff I obviously know nothing about, that made him who he was when we saw him. What we saw on the outside was the result of what was going on inside him—and that yearly shedding of his external defining feature had no bearing on his identity.

The same is true with us who have God's Spirit inside us. When we know Jesus Christ, He gives us identity through His Holy Spirit. When we have that, we have everything, no matter what prized earthly possessions we may lose.

SOUL SURGERY

When I kept silent, my bones wasted away.
PSALM 32:3

After two decades of ministry, I've learned something about every one of us walking the planet: we all have things going on inside us that need to be treated in order to be healed. In some cases, that healing requires surgery—soul surgery.

Here's what I've also learned about soul surgery: it must be done in the light, never in the dark.

Here's the problem, though: those of us who carry around things inside of us, things that require soul surgery, have what seems to be an inborn need to keep those things—those problematic spiritual tumors—hidden from view. The reason is simple: we don't want people to know about the ugly things going on inside us—the struggle with unresolved anger, the habit of viewing pornography, or our battle with materialism. We're terrified what others might think of us if they knew. . . .

So we keep our sickness in the dark, hidden from view. We believe the lie that we can go on living healthy spiritual lives with these things hidden in the dark. God didn't create us to work that way.

David wrote that his body was wasting away from lack of confession. I've seen it myself, more times than I'd care to count, and I've learned this truth: silence kills the heart. When we keep things in the dark, the enemy finds it easier to lie to us all the more, because darkness distorts reality. The reality is that everybody has something going on in their lives. You are not really alone; you're just *choosing* to live alone by remaining silent.

The truth is, there are countless brothers in Christ who have "been there," who can walk you through your surgery, and who will show you more grace, more hope, and more practical truths than you can imagine. . .if you'll only let them know your heart.

THROWIN' A FIT

In the South, we use phrases that make sense to Southerners but not to anyone else, often because those phrases have multiple meanings, all based on the context in which we employ them.

For instance, we often say, "Bless his heart." That can indicate sincere sympathy for someone we know is struggling, but it can also be a kind, Southern way of saying someone is "a moron wrapped in an idiot" without using such harsh language.

We also use phrases like "He threw a fit," which can mean some fella was smoldering with anger. It can also indicate intense joy, as when a person just launches out with a tub full of happy and pours it all over everyone without bias or reservation.

We're told more than once that Jesus "rejoiced greatly." In fact, we're told in Luke 10:21 that He "rejoiced greatly in the Holy Spirit" (NASB). I think Jesus was all sorts of happy because His Father's plan was coming together. He could see everything moving forward for His Father's vision, and it jolted Him. I have no doubt He threw a fit. . .of joy.

I'm not just writing for dramatic effect when I say I believe we get the joy side of Jesus all wrong. Let me illustrate.

I have two boys, and when they were little, I'd watch how they would interact with people—and learn a lot about those of us who call ourselves "adults."

My boys would basically ignore or shy away from sour people. I don't blame them, because kids are not drawn to sour people. Yet we know that children approached Jesus. In fact, large crowds of people followed Jesus. This I know: crowds do not tend to follow killjoys—not unless something is mixed in the Kool-Aid making them do it.

I think we get the joy of Jesus wrong because we cannot see Jesus eating chips and salsa just before shooting bottle rockets on a holiday. We get the joy of Jesus all wrong because we focus on the man who condemned the Pharisees and not on the man who talked Zacchaeus down out of a tree. Have you ever seen a short, fat, grown man trying to climb a tree? You know that had to be a hilarious sight. Jesus had to be laughing at the circus before Him.

Few things are more toxic to the human spirit than repressed joy. Sadly, we Christians know we should be happy, but we are afraid to be too happy. And we're especially afraid to be too happy in church, where we're around other Jesus people who are supposed to be happy themselves. In church, of course, of all places, if you get too happy and start "rejoicing greatly in the Holy Spirit," then people just might call you names.

Let's not be afraid to "throw a fit" of joy, even if others think it's strange to do so. After all, we have Jesus—and He gives us all the reason we need.

GOD AND HOOTSUITE

I learned pretty quickly that ministry isn't a lot of fun for people who need a consistent stream of affirmation. Sure, people continually encourage me in many ways, but I can tell you that man cannot live on encouragement alone, for it normally comes in small doses.

In fact, of all people, those of us in ministry receive little energy derived from ROI: return on investment. The reason is simple: a lot of what we do is measured in the eternal scope—which means that much of the fruit of our life's work will not show up in what we can see in the here and now.

Few things can cause a man of God to wither faster than living in a barren land where encouragement is scarce. We are human and, like it or not, we are created to be emotional. Our souls need injections of encouragement, no matter how strong we may be as leaders.

God recently spoke to me about this very issue. God has spoken to me through songs, through people, through creation, even through dreams. He had never spoken to me in the way He did most recently. God spoke to me about the results of the work of those of us called to ministry using, wait for it. . .Hootsuite.

Hootsuite is a social media manager that allows you to schedule out your tweets, Facebook posts, and other social media postings months ahead of time. Some people don't like Hootsuite, but if you write or produce videos for the sake of engaging men spiritually (like I do), then something like Hootsuite can be an incredible time saver.

Hootsuite has a "link shrinking" tool that allows you to simply put your link on your website page, where the video or article is living, and "shrink" it so that it becomes an "ow.ly" link. I know you've seen that, or maybe a "bit.ly" link, if you're on Twitter or Facebook. Ow.ly and bit.ly are the same sort of idea. They are link trackers.

The reason an "ow.ly" link is critical is that Hootsuite tracks performance for you. I can take an article or video from my website and post that link to Twitter, Facebook, or an email, and by using the "ow.ly" tracker, I can know exactly how many people have read it or watched it.

I'm not kidding when I say that ow.ly has changed my life and my perspective.

For a year or so, I wondered if what I was posting on Twitter or Facebook was actually helping people. I'd see a comment or two, a few retweets, or twenty or so "likes" on Facebook, but that was about it.

Until I purchased Hootsuite Pro. In the first week I used it, I was stunned.

I'd post an article and see only one or two retweets, but I'd pull up the tracker in Hootsuite Pro and see that 78 people had read it. I'd pull up another article or video link and see that 432 people had clicked on it. I had no idea that was happening until I had a device that tracked my results behind the curtain.

Never forget this simple reality when it comes to serving the Lord and living out your calling: you have no clue how far your life and your life's work are reaching and you never will . . .until you cross the river.

Don't track your work based on what you can see, because God didn't call you to measure your worth to Him in that way. You have an "ow.ly" tracker, and it is the God of the universe. He doesn't measure your analytics in the here and now because He knows better.

One day, you'll cross the river. On that day, my brother, you will be stunned at how He used you.

Do. Not. Quit.

SOMETHING YOU SHOULD EXPECT

*"For that is how their
ancestors treated the prophets."*
Luke 6:23

Jesus made it very clear to His followers that they would be hated simply because of being attached to His name. His name is enough to cause such conviction that His followers would be hated via association.

We Jesus followers were never given license to be theological snobs. Yet my fear is that Christians across America have been duped into the line of thinking that we cannot take stands for truth because the Gospel would be hindered by what would be seen as our opposition mentality.

If you're a Jesus follower, then you're going to face opposition for the stands you take. I'd rather be known as a voice shouting in the darkness while simultaneously holding a light than to sit silent in the darkness while feeling the numbing comfort of knowing I have a flashlight in my pocket.

SLOW DOWN

One of my most memorable golf teachers—aside from my father, who was a PGA professional—once told me, "Jason, it is far better to take thirty minutes and hit fifteen balls on the range with a purpose and a plan, than to hit an entire bucket of balls in ten minutes with no goal other than you went to the driving range today."

I've learned to take the same kind of approach to reading scripture. I've learned through simple observation that I get far more from the Bible when I slow down, read carefully, and try to get more out of every word I read.

I have tried to build into muscle memory a habit that when I open my Bible I pray something akin to, *Lord, slow down my mind. There is nothing more important in my life today than what I'm about to do in the next few minutes, so please help me to take the time to soak it all in.*

I'm telling you, it works. I close my eyes, slow down my heart, and then engage myself in the scriptures.

THE ONE THAT GOT AWAY

*Whoever disregards discipline comes to poverty
and shame, but whoever heeds correction is honored.*
PROVERBS 13:18

When I was nine years old, I had my eyes, and my heart, concretely fixed upon a new BB gun. The new pump-action gun was a major step up from my Daisy lever action, and I wanted one. I can still hear my dad laying out the conditions: "Pull the weeds growing in your grandfather's garden, and I'll buy you the BB gun you've been wanting."

Sounds easy, unless you knew my grandfather. My grandfather did nothing halfway. By the best estimate of my nine-year-old mind, I figured the garden to be approximately 237 acres of corn, beans, okra, tomatoes, and squash. It was hot outside, and on top of that, weeding and debugging that garden seemed like nothing short of prison labor. This was about a week's worth of work, but after only three hours at work, I found myself exhausted.

Halfway through, I decided I'd done enough to earn that BB gun. I quickly pulled a few weeds from the rest of the garden and called for my dad to come inspect my efforts. "Sorry, son," he said. "That's nowhere close to finished." Dad actually did let me quit, and I never got that BB gun.

Love doesn't mean that I'm entitled to get whatever I want. My dad loved me too much to let me think I could cheat my way through a contract and yet somehow reap an honest reward.

THE LONG KNOCKER

Gracious words are a honeycomb,
sweet to the soul and healing to the bones.
PROVERBS 16:24

His moniker was "the Long Knocker," a nickname he humorously and ironically self-applied because he was normally fifty yards behind any golfer in his foursome when it came to tee shots.

Mr. Welch may not have held the ability to compress the golf ball as strongly as others in his crew, but there was one area where no man was his equal. From his lips came nothing but encouraging words—very intentional, precise, encouraging words.

As a young golfer, I spent an incredible amount of time on the range. So did Mr. Welch. We became pals. No matter how I was hitting the ball, no matter what my most recent tournament score revealed about the status of my game, Mr. Welch would tell me, with intense specificity, how he thought I was playing the game so very well.

There were times I knew that he knew I wasn't playing well at all. It didn't matter, though. All I knew was that Bobby Welch was *for* me. *No matter what.* His words of encouragement were, at times, injections of life placed perfectly into my heart.

BILL GATES' MONEY

I do not have the kind of money Bill Gates has, and I'm not sure I'd want it. That's a massive level of responsibility and stress. But I have dreamed many times about what I'd do if I *did* have that kind of money. I know I would first make sure my boys and my wife would be set for life. Then I'd do the same for my parents and Michelle's parents. The same is true for the rest of my family.

There was a time when that's where it would stop for me. Now I know what I would do after that.

Some time back, I went on a mission trip to Moldova, a poverty-stricken country that was part of the former Soviet Union, to work with orphans through a ministry called Justice and Mercy International (JMI), one of the most hands-on global justice ministries I've ever seen.

While hard facts are difficult to determine because trafficking is so secretive, empirical research from human relief organizations does show that up to 70 percent of orphaned boys, once kicked out of the orphanage at age fifteen, end up arrested for survival crimes. Empirical evidence from the late 1990s to early 2000s indicates that up to 70 percent of orphaned girls, once kicked out of the orphanage at age fifteen, were trafficked into the sex slave trade.

So if I had Bill Gates's money, I'd work with JMI to help fulfill its vision of building even more transition homes than they already have to help kids once they are put out on the street.

I don't have Bill Gates' money, but my wife, Michelle, and I do have $40 a month to sponsor a child. Through JMI, I can literally go back to Moldova, hug a child's neck, touch the clothes I've provided for her, and see the hope in her eyes that comes from knowing that somebody in America loves her—knows her, writes to her, and comes back to see her.

In the end, it's not about having Bill Gates' money; it's about being faithful with my money to do what I can do. That's realistic, and it's possible. *(For more information about JMI, visit justiceandmercy.org.)*

THE VOICE OF THE PEOPLE

Take delight in the L<small>ORD</small>,
and he will give you the desires of your heart.
P<small>SALM</small> 37:4

Blessed are they that shout,
for they shall be heard.
1 J<small>ASON</small> 3:1

Smartphones are amazing devices—and I found they are very useful for a dad trying to partner with his son as the two devise a scheme to get the boy a foul ball at a baseball game.

By the time Cole and I arrived at the ballpark on this given night, it had been raining for hours. I told Cole there was a small chance the rain would stop just in time for the first inning, leaving the ballpark virtually empty because so many fans would assume the game was rained out. The Triple-A affiliate of the Milwaukee Brewers is the Nashville Sounds, and they were playing the Omaha Storm—a fitting mascot on a rainy night.

We were sitting by the first base dugout, so we created a plan. Using our iPhonic resources, we searched the web and found the Omaha Storm's website, seeking to uncover the first baseman's name. Our father-son scheme to get Cole a baseball was for him to make his quest personal by screaming the player's name as he ran to the dugout.

We discovered quickly that Omaha's first baseman (his first name was Clint) was a softy, for he continually gave baseball after baseball to little girls in the stands. Then something unexpected happened.

Unbeknownst to me, an unseen force had permeated the crowd, but no one was talking about it. In the sixth inning, Cole once again went down to the dugout to hold up his arms with his little baseball glove in hand while shouting the first baseman's name. This time, however, when Cole opened his mouth to shout his name, the *entire* crowd on the first base side of the stadium started shouting in unison, "Clint! Clint! Clint!" as they pointed to Cole.

Cole opened up his mouth, but sixty voices filled the air, making his voice thunder like one of the apocalyptic four horsemen—so much so that Clint, who had his eyes on yet another blond-headed dress wearer, turned to the source of the clamor, only to find himself staring straight into the eyes of a little boy with his glove held high.

When the ball rolled across the roof of the dugout, my son swallowed it up like a vacuum cleaner on jet fuel. The entire first base side went nuts.

MY OWN COSMIC BILLBOARD

Be transformed by the
renewing of your mind.
ROMANS 12:2

We've all got our last nerve, that raw place where people don't know how sensitive we are to something until they step on it. I try not to have many places in my heart where a last nerve resides bare and exposed. Even still, I'd be lying if I said there were no spots in my life where I can go from zero to sixty on the speedometer of angry.

One such place is when I must put up with a person who has proven, over and over again, that he has embraced a bad attitude as his mode of living. I realize that every one of us will have seasons (actually more than once if we live long enough) when our attitude is broken down like an old truck on the side of the road.

Here's the issue: life can and will bring all kinds of stuff my way to quickly attack my attitude. The problem is, attitude affects everything. Attitude is the game changer, but it changes the game only in ways I *allow* or *want* it to be changed.

When Jesus changes a heart, He transforms the whole person. His cosmic grace, power, strength, and joy soak through our spiritual and emotional DNA with no strand uncovered. My attitude is my witness to a lost and dying world that my joy, my hope, and my grace for living out each and every situation are not up for sale to the highest bidder of circumstance.

WHAT A BROTHER *WON'T* DO

Don't be deceived,
my dear brothers and sisters.
JAMES 1:16

Because the apostle James uses the word *brother* so very often in his letter, you cannot read his descriptions of how to live out the faith without filtering them through the connection of brotherhood. This is about kinship and family. As my friends in Mississippi say, "How's ya mama 'n' them?" Family matters.

James gets to this place where he goes straight to the bone of how brothers are to live, then, in the light of what it means to have kinfolk in the name of Jesus: "Those who consider themselves religious and yet do not keep a tight rein on their tongues deceive themselves, and their religion is worthless" (James 1:26).

If you are the least bit concerned with having a solid understanding of God's Word, then there are nonnegotiable rules you must follow when it comes to interpreting the scriptures. One of these basic fundamentals is the fact that you cannot just read a passage in context—that is, what comes directly before and after it. You must go further and read the passage in light of the entire book in which it's recorded.

To get a tight grip on what James 1:26 is all about, you must understand it in light of all he's saying about God, life, faith. . .and brotherhood. This way you can see what he's getting at when he talks about the tongue as it fits together as a whole, not just as a chapter.

Then it becomes all too clear: brothers do not slander brothers.

THE GOAL OF WISDOM

If any of you lacks wisdom, you should ask God, who gives generously to all without finding fault, and it will be given to you.
JAMES 1:5

Praying for wisdom is one of those prayers for which God promises to give you exactly what you want. The point of God granting you wisdom is not just so you'll make better decisions that ultimately honor His name—as important as that is. His grand design in granting you wisdom is so you will know His heart in ways you didn't before.

I do not have a favorite scripture. In my top three, however, is a prayer Paul prays for his friends in Ephesus: "I keep asking that the God of our Lord Jesus Christ, the glorious Father, may give you the Spirit of wisdom and revelation, so that you may know him better" (Ephesians 1:17).

A spirit of wisdom and revelation: the ability to see beyond the surface, to see what is actually there instead of what appears to be there.

So that you may know Him better: the goal of being granted the favor of wisdom and revelation—knowing the heart of a God who *always* has your best interests in mind.

SHORT-TERM GAINS

See that no one is sexually immoral,
or is godless like Esau, who for a single meal
sold his inheritance rights as the oldest son.
HEBREWS 12:16

Bad decisions often look even worse after you've had a few years to think back on what you did in that one moment. The story of Jacob and Esau carries with it a ton of dynamics, yet one that sticks out is that Esau would be willing to sell his "birthright" for a meal.

Like many of you who read *The Man Minute*, Esau loved to hunt. The difference was he hunted to survive while we hunt for sport. One day, Esau came home from a hunt and he was, as the Bible puts it, "famished." Jacob was cooking up some stew and told his brother he'd share it—but only if Esau granted him his birthright.

The birthright was no small thing, for these men were sons of Isaac, who was the son of Abraham. A birthright included all the benefits of the family name, and with a family name like Abraham, this would be a birthright you'd want to keep. But Esau let his physical desires drive his thinking and made the deal with Jacob. It was a short-term gain for a long-term loss.

At its core, this is the very nature of all temptation. It's the masking of the truth that sin has consequences. We accept the offer of temporary relief or pleasure, even though we know there will be long-term ramifications.

How many times have you looked back on something you've done and wished you'd never done it? One way you can avoid this kind of regret is to stop and think before you act. The next time you're faced with a choice you know could carry long-term negative consequences, step back and ask yourself if it's a wise choice. Keep the end you know God has for you in mind, and you'll be able to honor Him through the choices you make.

SUPPRESSION

*Always be prepared to give an answer to everyone
who asks you to give the reason for the hope that
you have. But do this with gentleness and respect.*
1 PETER 3:15

I have always found it odd that the Bible tells us we are to "defend" the Gospel. I do not feel a need to defend God or His truths—as if He or His words are vulnerable to demise.

Who is able to defend such splendor as that of our Creator God in a manner worthy to do Him justice? It simply cannot be done. Mere mortals must bow the will to His reality, and refusing to do so is the epitome of arrogance and worthy of divine judgment.

I understand, though, that Christians should be able, ready, and willing to make a case for the faith. The apostle Peter tells us to have a ready defense; that is, to be prepared to "give the reason" why we believe.

Whether or not he wants to, every man must reckon with the truth of who God is and what He has said. It's commonly thought that when a person denies Christ, he does so on the basis of the rejection of facts that a Christ follower presents. But when someone denies Christ, he does so not by rejecting facts, but by suppressing truth.

God created in every heart the ability to accept His reality, and when someone denies that reality, he isn't rejecting Him from the outside in, but from the inside out.

This truth is at the heart of what the apostle Paul meant when he wrote, "The wrath of God is being revealed from heaven against all the godlessness and wickedness of people, who suppress the truth by their wickedness, since what may be known about God is plain to them, because God has made it plain to them" (Romans 1:18–19).

INTOXICATED BY SURPRISE

Beyond question, my favorite time of the year is spring. From mid-March to mid-May, when strutters are on the troll, I find myself obsessed with the chase.

I recently introduced one of my soul brothers to the addiction that runs through my veins. He asked for it, and though I fully warned him about the potential life changes that could ensue, even still he chose to enter the woods with me. Two hours later, Russ Rankin was staring down the barrel of a shotgun and introducing his first tom turkey to a mouthful of #6 turkey loads.

Walking out of the woods with me, bird in tow, he looked over and said, "You know, I've always understood why guys would love to hunt trophy bucks because of the big antlers, but I can see how this would totally capture a man. It's because of the 'game' you play, isn't it?"

At that moment, I knew Russ needed no further mentoring in the world of feathered fever. In the span of the 120 minutes it took to bag this bird and throw it over his shoulder, the seductive sounds of the gobble and yelp had saturated his marrow.

When I enter the woods to chase a tom, I never know the outcome. I will get up at 3:30 a.m. and then spend the day battling intense humidity, ticks, the possibility of stepping on a copperhead, and the likelihood of coming home empty-handed just to experience the drama of a journey with no guaranteed outcome.

I'm convinced that the secret of why countless numbers of men are so uninterested in the idea of "church" has to do with the fact that they see the Christian faith as devoid of surprises. A. W. Tozer once said that we've reduced God to someone who will "never surprise us, never astonish us, never overwhelm us, nor ever transcend us."

Your personal faith journey can look just like the hunt of a lifetime, and that constant sense of adventure alive in your own life can have transforming effects on the people around you. Jesus never once called a man to a predictable, boring life lived under a steeple. He calls us to a relationship, and every relationship has ever-changing dynamics.

Oh that we could lead people in our churches to settle for nothing less than faith journeys that scoff at the idea of rote approaches to the eternal God who has made Himself accessible through Jesus the Christ. And may we forever be on a quest to experience the astonishment of His great surprises.

THE HOLY REMINDER

"But the Advocate, the Holy Spirit, whom the Father
will send in my name, will teach you all things and
will remind you of everything I have said to you."
JOHN 14:26

If you were to read the above verse using different translations of the Bible, you'd find that the Holy Spirit is called
several different names: Advocate, Helper, Counselor, and
Comforter. In John 14:17 Jesus calls the Holy Spirit the
"Spirit of truth," which points to His role as a great supernatural filter who keeps us from believing lies about God,
about ourselves, about our circumstances, or about the people
around us.

Jesus also spoke about one of the roles of the Holy Spirit
that for some reason dropped off my radar in past readings
of John. Jesus tells us that the Spirit will "will remind you of
everything I have said to you" (John 14:26).

To me, that is a game changer, for it tells me that in
those times when my mind is dull, confused, or simply un-
responsive due to my humanity, the Spirit will remind me of
the truths of God's faithfulness so that I may navigate the
journey of manhood.

I look back on my life and see time after time when God,
through His Spirit, brought to the forefront of my mind moments when He's proven Himself sovereign. The next time
that happens, I can realize it's not just God the Father at work
in my life; it's literally His Spirit doing for me what I cannot
do myself.

SENDERO LUMINOSO (SPANISH FOR "SHINING PATH")

Two are better than one, because they have a good return for their labor: If either of them falls down, one can help the other up. But pity anyone who falls and has no one to help them up.
ECCLESIASTES 4:9–10

While filming a hunt for the Record Book Project, my soul brother Jeremy Harrill and I were able to roll tape at the legendary Tecomate Ranch in south Texas. The culmination of the trip came during the last evening, when a really nice 10-pointer emerged in the sendero. My heart rate spiked. He was not the largest whitetail I'd ever taken, but my eyes widened because I knew I was about to pull the trigger on closing out this piece of the project.

Once the smoke cleared, I was in disbelief. Most of the time after my muzzleloader explodes, I see antlers on the ground. But on this cloudless evening, all I saw was Texas scrub brush as I lowered the end of my barrel.

I felt sick to my stomach. I had no idea what the deer had done postshot, for the thick tangle of limbs and brush lining the sendero had swallowed up any chance of even getting a glimpse of him. I felt as if I had miserably failed the team, my guide, my cameraman and his church, and everyone who'd ever supported the Record Book Project.

Our guide, Bruce, was an incredibly patient man, and he had quickly proven that he was involved in this project for one reason: to help us turn the page on this part of the story.

Finding only two dime-sized spots of blood, we decided not to push it. I was now spiraling into the worst abyss known to every big-game hunter—that moment when he knows, based on past experience, that odds are he's seen the last of that set of antlers.

I sat speechless, staring into the night as we prepared to head back to the lodge to review the footage. Then Bruce came to the truck. Every great guide knows this is not a good moment to say much of anything to your hunter. Bruce, leaning just inside the threshold of the window, looked at me and communicated, with simple and precise words of encouragement, that the fight was far from over when it came to finding this buck.

Reviewing the footage at the kitchen table later on, we saw that my shot was far better than I'd realized. In one of the most humbling moments of my three decades of hunting, I observed that each one of the Tecomate guides was quietly strapping on his gear. Though by no means required to, every one of them was intent on going back to the path, now gleaming with a white December moon, to help me find the buck.

It was the classiest gesture within the brotherhood of hunters I've ever seen.

Seven minutes later, and fifty yards into the thick country, I heard Mark, one of the Tecomate guides, yell out, "We've got a dead deer over here!"

Bruce extended his hand to congratulate me. Having now run the entire flywheel of human emotion, I knew I could do far better than a handshake. As I reached out to hug him, my brother from Montana said, "I'm not much of a hugger."

"I don't really care, Bruce," were the only words that rose up from my heart. Hunting camp or not, surrounded by men or by no one, I was hugging Bruce, for he had guided me with excellence.

Some paths in life are clad in cacti and dust that tear your world apart. Some are laced with moments of indescribable joy. I had experienced both in a matter of three rotations of the clock. Bruce and his brotherhood of guides were willing to settle for nothing less than illuminating the path for my journey, in order that they might be their brother's keeper.

"DON'T JUDGE ME"

"Do not judge, or you too will be judged. For in the same way you judge others, you will be judged, and with the measure you use, it will be measured to you. Why do you look at the speck of sawdust in your brother's eye and pay no attention to the plank in your own eye?"

MATTHEW 7:1–3

It's an attitude now as much a part of American culture as apple pie and baseball. What Jesus intended as a warning for His followers to refrain from making harsh and incomplete assessments about someone's character is now taken to basically mean, "You don't have the right to tell me when I'm wrong, no matter what I'm doing."

Do Christians have a right to judge others? The answer, as uncomfortable as it makes people in our culture, is: absolutely! The problem, however, is found in how we define the word *judgment*.

What about Jesus' words, "Do not judge, or you too will be judged"? Was Jesus saying that we as His followers don't have the right—or the ability—to gather information about others (and ourselves) and then come to solid, biblical conclusions? Far from it!

In the same passage in which Jesus appears to be telling believers never to make judgments about the behaviors and attitudes of others, He said of false prophets, "By their fruit you will recognize them" (Matthew 7:16). Thus, you'll know to stay away from false prophets because you have made biblical assessments of what they say and do. That's judgment in its truest form.

So what was Jesus getting at when He warned against judging others? His warning was actually against spiritually immature judgment, which is when you make character assessments based on your own assumptions and incomplete information. I have to confess that every time I've made that mistake, I ended up far off the mark in my own assessments of others.

Jesus' point is this: never make assumptions about another person's character based on limited information or interaction. When we do that, we end up "judging" others based on comparisons to our own lives—and that leads us to the idea of being aware of "the plank in your own eye." The standard of measure is important here, for it keeps us from demonstrating an attitude of, "Well, my life isn't perfect, but at least I'm not like him." That's a spiritually immature conclusion, and it leads to the kind of judgmental spirit Jesus warned us against.

Now let's flip the page. Perhaps you know a believer who has repeatedly demonstrated a horrible temperament. Over and over again, this person explodes in anger—even though he carries the name of Christ. One day you summon the courage to talk to this man and tell him that you see in him a consistent, toxic character trait—one that leads to damaging attitudes and actions. Are you judging that man when you tell him you have observed that he has an issue with anger? No! You're simply pointing out—in a spirit of love—that this man's outbursts of anger are not consistent with someone who has the Spirit of the living God inside him.

The bottom line is that Jesus gave us guidelines for how to make righteous assessments. Our part as brothers in Christ is to examine our own hearts and ask ourselves if we're lashing out at a person based on our own assumptions . . .or if we're speaking out of true love and concern because we want to restore him to a better walk with God.

Never confuse telling the truth with being harshly judgmental. No matter what the world may tell you, neither God nor any of His followers is bound to our culture's definition of truth and righteousness.

ROI

Do not be deceived: God cannot be mocked. A man reaps what he sows. Whoever sows to please their flesh, from the flesh will reap destruction; whoever sows to please the Spirit, from the Spirit will reap eternal life. Let us not become weary in doing good, for at the proper time we will reap a harvest if we do not give up.
GALATIANS 6:7–9

The phrase "return on investment" (ROI for short)—or variations of it—is built into every man's vocabulary, and it's what drives almost every decision we make, both personally and professionally. We want to know that our work, our decisions, and our efforts will pay off for us in the end. Therefore, we measure our success by a return on investment.

Success is a moving target, because every individual, every company, every business, and every industry measures growth by different standards. Success is important, but the real question is, "How do we define success?"

The scriptures tell us that if we sow in the flesh—another word for the carnal nature—we'll reap the worst the flesh can offer, but if we sow in things eternal, we will reap a harvest straight from the heart of God.

Most of us have employers—or at least people we must answer to—but our attitude is to be that our work is for the Lord. God does measure success, but His measurements may not pay out a tangible dividend here on earth. If you choose to plant in eternal fields, you can know that you are guaranteed a return that is beyond anything in the here and now.

I'd say that's the greatest return on our investments we dare hope for!

MY REPRESSED SELF

I never saw the members of my family's
church enjoying themselves.
FRIEDRICH NIETZSCHE

When Cole, my oldest son, was only five years old, he taught me mountains of wisdom about worship. One day in church, the band started cranking the music and Cole started clapping his hands—even though nobody else was clapping, for it wasn't really a clapping-type song. That didn't stop my boy, though. He started clapping his hands just because the mood hit him.

Then, out of the corner of my eye, I saw two small hands stretched out toward the heavens. Cole was a hand-clapping, hand-raising five-year-old, just singing away and praising God.

My heart was full that day because my son had no idea what others might have said about how he should worship God. He just knew he was happy, and he wanted to show God he was happy—and in a way that made sense to his five-year-old mind.

To be candid with you, I know that there are times when I am repressed when it comes to worshipping the Lord. That's because I am too concerned about what someone else may think of me.

Here's what I've learned about reverence: it's a state of the heart, an attitude. Church culture has always taught me that reverence is about trying not to offend God by wearing the wrong clothes, or by making too much noise when you sing, or by moving around too much when you sing songs to Him—because if God sees you moving and grooving,

He's gonna hammer you for it.

I've come to the conclusion that a man can come to church in an Armani suit, wearing a Rolex watch, and place a large check in the offering plate...and yet still be a foul stench in the nostrils of God. Reverence might have a tiny bit to do with dress codes and traditions, but it has far more to do with being set free to worship God from the heart.

The worst thing I could have done is shut Cole down when he was worshipping God, for that would have taught him that God was not a fan of his happy self. Whether he fully understood what he was doing in the moment didn't matter to me. What mattered most was that he was free to worship in a way that made sense to him.

That day, sitting beside my son, I saw firsthand what liberated worship looks like. And it was beautiful.

REBELLION IN DISGUISE?

Sometimes I go through seasons when my prayer life is just off. Plain and simple, I neglect spending time with God. I pull out of it, but then it happens again. You can probably identify with the story.

It's natural to have ups and downs in all matters of the Spirit. I think that's why Jesus didn't let Peter, James, and John stay on the mountain where He was transfigured. After all, where can a man go from there? Once you've seen that, you've pretty much seen all you need to see. Either you go on to glory, or you go back down the mountain.

Life was intended to be lived on the peaks, in the valleys, and in all the in-betweens. You cannot live on the mountain every single day. I get that.

I think I'm sometimes too quick to chalk up my lack of God conversations to the natural ebb and flow of the world. I think my neglect to pray is, in its truest sense, rebellion. It's me wanting to live life on my own terms, and in the end, it's not only immature but dangerous.

FEAR

Fear is a four-letter word that's likely at the root of more of your decisions than you might think. If you examine your life closely, you just might find that fear, not faith, is the fuel that drives your direction. Fear is easily disguised in statements that float through your mind like, *Well, the logical thing to do would be...* Sometimes you see it manifested in lies floating to the surface of your spirit, such as, *God would never cause you to put at risk...*

While it's true that God has given us brains with which to grow in Christlike wisdom, our enemy, Satan, often counteracts righteous adventures using the guise of logic.

When you read the Bible, you'll see that God often defies logic and common sense. It wasn't logical for Noah to build a boat when he'd never before seen rain. And it made no sense when God told Abraham to put his son on an altar.

What I'm learning is that in life I must make a choice about the love of God. I can trust His love, or I can make a counteroffer to that love—which, if I am honest with myself, is always an attempt to control the outcome. If God is love, and if He loves me, then I have no reason to fear for my future.

The following passage speaks to this truth. You might want to read it several times this week. . .slowly:

This is how love is made complete among us so that we will have confidence on the day of judgment: In this world we are like Jesus. There is no fear in love. But perfect love drives out fear, because fear has to do with punishment. The one who fears is not made perfect in love.
1 John 4:17–18

BEING "THE MAN"

Such confidence we have through Christ before God. Not that
we are competent in ourselves to claim anything for ourselves,
but our competence comes from God. He has made us
competent as ministers of a new covenant—not of the letter
but of the Spirit; for the letter kills, but the Spirit gives life.

2 Corinthians 3:4-6

Most every guy I've ever met has a deep need to be "the man"—not necessarily out of ego, but out of a need to think of himself as competent when it comes to navigating life's challenges.

I include myself in this appraisal. The desire to see myself as competent has become a big part of the driving force within me to excel. However, when left unfiltered by the Word of God, my desire to be a competent man can become a deadly toxin that infects my heart, clouds my perspective, and warps my relationships.

Over and over again, I've had to force myself to understand the eternal truth that there's truly nothing I can do to make myself a fully competent man. I cannot be educated enough, wealthy enough, or smart enough to handle life on every level. I've come to understand that thinking I can achieve that level of competence is, in its truest form, a carnal approach to life.

Here's what makes me truly competent: the fact that I'm in Christ, the fact that I'm washed in the blood of His eternal covenant. It's "Christ in me, the hope of glory" that makes me competent.

My own competence is tainted with far less than God's best. My ability to try to be "the man" is only as good as the depth to which I know *the Man*. Knowing that truth allows me to live life without the bondage of having to perform, for my performance is measured only by whether I am grafted into the great I Am.

LEARN AND REST

"Come to me, all you who are weary and burdened, and I will give you rest. Take my yoke upon you and learn from me, for I am gentle and humble in heart, and you will find rest for your souls."
MATTHEW 11:28-29

The further I go in my journey with Christ, the more I find that faith is every bit as much a mental game as it is a matter of the heart. Faith is about how you look at your world; it's about how you interpret the things life throws at you daily. Faith is about knowing something is true, not believing that something is *most likely* true.

I've read the above passage countless times, but one day it struck me that Jesus told me to "learn" from Him.

So the question becomes, *Learn what?*

Is there a connection between learning and resting?

It seems to me that the closer a man gets to the heart of the God who created him, the more he learns what it means to walk by faith and not by sight. Learning is a life-long progression. A man must learn that God is faithful, and that assurance comes only over a period of interpreting life, waiting, and watching as God comes through, over and over again. I learn, based on experiences in everyday life, that He is more than able.

I believe that what Jesus meant by "learn from Me" is that He wants me to learn that He is perfectly faithful—that He cannot lie, that He cannot foul up, and that He cannot lead me in a wrong direction.

When I learn that He truly is sovereign in every single situation of my life, then I can find "rest" for my soul and for my emotions, because I have learned that in every situation, He is who He said He is—faithful.

SOCIAL MEDIA AND FRUITLESS DISCUSSION

Some men, straying from these things,
have turned aside to fruitless discussion.
1 Timothy 1:6 NASB

Social media is just that: social. It's about a free exchange of life and, sometimes, the exchange of ideas.

However, I've learned something about dealing with people who have different worldviews than my own on social media. I often feel compelled to dispel a myth or counter a political opinion on social media, but I've discovered that doing so is usually pointless and almost never ends well.

The apostle Paul instructed Timothy, a young guy trending toward the pastoral fraternity, that the goal of instruction is love, good conscience, and sincere faith (1 Timothy 1:5). This was during a time when those opposing Paul based their assertions on life, as well as their views about God, on cultural trends.

Paul follows that by warning Timothy to stay away from "fruitless discussion," for it never pays off and only leaves people confused and angry. For me, the hard part about following Paul's advice is knowing what's fruitless and what isn't.

I can tell you this: so often when I engage in a civil exchange with people in a conversation on Twitter, it gets ugly—and quickly. I think that's because many people use social media to make blanket statements without having to engage in civil debate. Like a Batman punch on Twitter, it's akin to "Blam! Here's my say, so deal with it!"

Be careful that you don't waste time on fruitless conversations. . .especially on social media.

ABANDONING RETAIL

If you'd asked me a year ago what I believed are the greatest challenges facing churches today, I'd have offered up an answer having to do with how we fail to "do church" in a way that makes sense in our modern culture. I would have stated that while our message must never change, our approaches to ministry must *always* be changing.

Today, however, if you were to ask me the same question, I'd bring you a simpler answer. I am now convinced that what is missing in churches today is not simply a better way to do ministry. What's missing in our churches is favor—God's favor.

The New Testament church we read about in the book of Acts had no money, no technology, no marketing plan, no children's ministry, and no ministers with postgraduate degrees. All of those things can be wonderful assets in ministry today, but the New Testament church had none of them, and yet that small band of Holy Spirit–fueled believers radically changed the world and the culture around them.

Churches in America today have everything they need and then some, but we pose little if no threat to our culture. I believe that's because we're missing the favor God gave His people in New Testament times.

We can't buy favor with money. Favor comes from God, and He gives it to churches who want it more than they want a campus other churches would envy. Favor comes when people who fill the pews are more interested in God's presence than in simply presenting a retail form of Christianity that gives folks the ability to shop for a church like they're shopping at Target.

Favor is the Bethel to which we must return. Without it, we can do everything we want to grow our churches, but we'll never grow a kingdom.

SOMETHING OF WORTH

I was fishing alone on what has become one of my favorite stretches of water, the Rio Grande in northern New Mexico. Along the Texas border, the Rio Grande is a muddy river, but it's entirely different in New Mexico and Colorado. It can be great water for large trout, but navigating this stream means traversing large boulders. In the fly-fishing world we call it "boulder hopping."

I clutched a large purple lava rock with my right hand to steady my descent to the water's edge, and as I looked down, I saw tucked on top of a streamside rock a lost treasure: an old toy truck. It was made for the entertainment of generations before me, and it was perched there almost as though someone had intentionally put it there on display. I'm fairly certain that the river had gently pushed it there over time, for no little feet ever walk near these fast waters.

I didn't know what to make of it, really. The first emotion I felt, for some odd reason, was sadness.

Being the father of sons, I thought of a little boy who'd been distracted and left his favorite toy truck by the river somewhere upstream, where the water runs more slowly and gently. The question ran through my soul, *Where are you today, brother?* I thought about the choices he'd made over time and how those choices had shaped his future.

That once bright red truck had seen better days. Still, it did have some value to someone—even if it was a long, long time ago.

My thoughts veered to something Jesus said:

> *"Suppose one of you has a hundred sheep and loses one of them. Doesn't he leave the ninety-nine in the*

open country and go after the lost sheep until he finds it? And
when he finds it, he joyfully puts it on his shoulders and goes
home. Then he calls his friends and neighbors together and
says, 'Rejoice with me; I have found my lost sheep.' "
LUKE 15:4-6

The whole point of chapter 15 of Luke is that something of value was lost, and the owner, though he had a surplus of the same missing item, went out to look for it and would not return until he found it.

Every man at some point feels alone and forsaken, as if his choices have caused him to float into places where the current is simply too strong, leaving his fate to the unknown. God, the difference maker, takes it upon Himself to search for, rescue, and restore us when we're lost. And this for one simple reason: every man has value to the owner.

FORCED TO DEAL WITH THE LIGHT

The Light shines in the darkness,
and the darkness did not comprehend it.
JOHN 1:5 NASB

A few fall hunting seasons ago, I was chasing what Indians called the "ghost of the timber." This elusive creature has other formal names, such as Wapiti, a Shawnee word meaning "white rump." This mighty ghost has held true to its name, for elk have proven themselves a formidable opponent for me thus far in my high-country journeys.

I wanted to get high into the timber on this particular November morning, so I left the cabin at 2:30 a.m. The walk would take three hours in the snow. The moon was perfectly full and the sky was completely clear. It was pure worship for me. There I was on the west slope of the Continental Divide, breathing in the clean, cold air. The moonlit travel at ten thousand feet made it seem as if I was mere inches from touching the face of God.

I stopped for some water, and as I reached into my pack, I happened to look up. Miles and miles away, on another range of the mountain chain, I saw another journeyman. It was about 3:30 by this time. He was on his way up his own set of timber, and he was using a modern-day horse: an ATV or, as they are sometimes called, a four-wheeler.

Though I was miles away, I could see his headlights, and two thoughts occurred to me. The first flash going through my tired mind was, *I bet elk love those things. They can see you coming for miles!* The second thought that stirred my mind was, *"The Light shines in the darkness, and the darkness did not comprehend it."*

There was no way *not* to see the light. I would literally have had to close my eyes tightly shut in order not to see it—and even then, the light would be on my mind. The light was piercing the black Colorado night, because that's what light does. In the midst of the darkness, the light put me in a position where I had to deal with it.

Jesus had a best friend named John. Read John's Gospel, and you'll see that he saw prisms of Jesus' life that could only be seen from close—*very* close—proximity.

So what does it say about the heart of a man—about the heart of humanity—when light pierces the darkness, but the darkness doesn't even know what it is? It tells me that the heart of every man is so saturated with darkness that he can't comprehend or recognize it. Which is why men need a Savior, why they need the Holy Spirit—to impart that power to humanity, for without a heavenly conduit, light would otherwise be overlooked, even in the darkest night.

SIGNS AND WET BOOTS

Do signs lead you to act in faith, or does faith move first, and then you'll see the signs? We often pray for God to give us a sign, but that's pretty much the reversal of what you'll find in biblical faith walking.

Just one example: God's people are at the edge of the Jordan River (see Joshua 3). They hear the water as it moves over the rocks and see the eddies swirl in places where the water runs deeper.

God doesn't command the people to stand and wait until the waters part before they cross. In fact, the scriptures tell us that "as soon as the priests who carried the ark reached the Jordan and their feet touched the water's edge, the water from upstream stopped flowing. It piled up in a heap. . . . The priests. . .stopped in the middle of the Jordan and stood on dry ground" (Joshua 3:15–17).

It wasn't until they started getting their feet wet that the waters parted, which means that every person had to commit to walking into the water with full anticipation that the waters would part at just the right time.

Slow down and think about that for a second.

When you are thrust into difficult situations and you have no idea what to do next, how do you respond? If you're wise, you do the only thing you know to do, given the information you have at the time.

When God places a burden on your heart, when He speaks to an area of your life in which He's calling you to wade in deeper, more often than not, that's all the information He'll give you—until you make that move onward.

God doesn't grant us a panoramic view of life—and that's for our own best interests. There's no faith involved with panoramic views. You grow when you glance down only to find that your boots are wet.

NOT JUST EMOTION

*"Therefore what God has joined together,
let no one separate."*
MARK 10:9

In 1997 I stood before God and man as I made a covenant promise to my wife, Michelle, that I'd love her, and her only, until death do us part.

Marriage is not easy. In fact, it's the hardest thing I've ever done. Marriage is tough. . .if you do it right.

Any marriage can be easy if the husband and wife simply coexist, don't really care about one another, or are merely living under the same rooftop. True love cannot live that way.

Yes, love is partly emotion, but at its core, love is grounded in a choice. Love is a promise kept, and only through kept promises do you find the anointing of God, for God never graces a fantasy. He only gives grace to that which is reality.

In God's grace, Michelle and I have stayed together, and by staying together, we have grown to love one another far more widely and deeply than we did in 1997. And it's beautiful.

I will keep my promise, and so will she.

YOUR ONE THING

A man who has become a mentor to me is a quiet pastor in a country church. We've known each other for years. He's a few years older than I am, but he's light-years ahead of me spiritually.

Over the years, Don has taught me so much about the life of a praying man. He recently told me that Old Testament followers rarely, if ever, prayed the way we pray now. We tend to pray in ways that closely resemble a grocery list of concerns. Not so with Jehovah-fearing Hebrews. They tended to pray for one thing, and that one thing consumed them so intensely that they prayed it through to the end.

Don calls it "your one thing."

Over time, I have learned to pray for my "one thing." Not long ago, God laid an issue on my heart, and that one thing was pretty much all I'd been sending heavenward for weeks thereafter. What has unfolded since has been an amazing jolt of spiritual awareness.

I started to see the hand of God moving, but in ways much smaller than before. Smaller? Yes, smaller. In the past, God would often have to do something loud and spectacular to get my attention. Now that I'm praying for my one thing until it comes to fruition, I find myself keenly aware of the smallest amount of His movement in this one area of my life. I watch for it, and I anticipate changes I need Him to make in me to see it through to completion.

God has my attention like never before, and that's the point of my conversations with Him. My heart cannot change unless I'm in a position to hear from Him.

When "one thing" is your target, then your aim has a much greater chance to be true.

READY

Over the years, I've developed the good habit of surrounding myself with a few men whose hearts are deep wells of wisdom and strength. One of those valiant brothers is a man named Pierce Marrs.

I have lunch with Pierce about once a month. At one of these meetings, we talked about fatherhood—specifically, about our sons' personalities. Pierce has two grown sons: Nick and Nathan. Pierce said that between the two boys, Nathan was the one who gravitated more toward science fiction, especially if it had anything to do with battles. In his younger years, Nathan loved to create battle scenes in which one could use swords, and that love for weaponry led to collecting various swords, which he actually learned to use quite well.

Pierce said that when Nathan was a young boy, at bedtime he would often take with him a sword and quietly place it by his bed. One night Pierce asked Nathan why he put a sword by his bed each night, and Nathan answered, "I just want to be ready."

While it may have been a young boy's imagination playing into the moment, Nathan's desire for readiness speaks mountains about the way his character was forming even as he slept—ready, prepared, anticipating a call that could come at any moment.

Great men of God are never formed by a passive approach to life. You won't find passivity in Moses or David. You certainly couldn't label Jonathan as possessing anything passive in his spirit. In the New Testament, Peter, Paul, John, and Mark were contemporaries who had that same caliber of heart.

These men changed the world, and their story is still

shaping our story today. That's how world changers do it: they take what they have been given and use it for the glory of God's greater cause.

World changers are, at all times, ready.

A SLAVE

"So if the Son makes you free,
you will be free indeed."
JOHN 8:36 NASB

The word *slavery* carries with it images of a blight on our history as Americans. Slaves own nothing, for they are owned. They are literally held in bondage to another owner's will. They have no real decision-making power, no ability to buy, sell, or trade. They have no ability to leverage their will on anything.

In the New Testament, the apostle Paul uses the same word to describe followers of Christ. When you decided to become a follower of Jesus, he says, you became a "slave" to God and His righteousness (see Romans 6).

Here's the paradox of this kind of slavery: when you are bound to Christ, you become chained to freedom. He is your owner, and your owner has set you free from the imprisonment created by a heart that was once bent toward self-destruction.

A true follower of Christ is a slave who understands that he owns nothing, understands that he has a Master and that his Master makes all the decisions. The difference is, those who are in bondage to Christ have been bound to the heart of God so that they no longer have to be tossed any which way the master of this world chooses for them to go.

We are bound to freedom, for it is truth that has set us free.

STANDARDS

Follow my example, as I follow the example of Christ.
1 CORINTHIANS 11:1

When my son Cole was five years old, we went to our first baseball game by ourselves. We'd been to several games before, but this time it was just us—and it was great.

The backstory is this: the Nashville Sounds, the Triple-A affiliate of the Milwaukee Brewers, down by two in the bottom of the ninth. . .two balls, two strikes, two outs, two men on. The first baseman at the time, Joe Koshansky, goes yard with a walk-off homer. The stadium went nuts!

Other than enjoying some time with my son, the best part of that day was getting to see one of my all-time favorite baseball players in person. Hall of Famer Ryne Sandberg, arguably the greatest second baseman of all time, was the manager of the Iowa Cubs, Nashville's opponent that day.

About halfway through the game I noticed something about Sandberg: he ran on and off the field each time he came out of the dugout. Then I began to observe how the rest of the team carried themselves. Every player and every coach hustled, and every player carried himself with honor in some small way you had to be looking for to notice. What really stood out to me was that each Cubs player wore his socks at the same height. No one player was doing his own thing. They looked like a ball club full of professionals.

It occurred to me that Sandberg had set the tone not just by telling his players what he expected of them, but also by modeling it for them. He held himself to the same standards he had set for his players, and he did it with class.

If we want to lead other men, we must model the same

kind of attitudes and actions we expect in others. And modeling these things involves far more than uttering catchphrases like "walking the walk." Modeling leadership is about allowing your convictions to so saturate your soul that everyone around you is affected by who you are and how you live.

MEASURING A MAN

"When people fall down, do they not get up?
When someone turns away, do they not return?"
JEREMIAH 8:4

Failures may be good measures of a man's decisions, but they don't always measure the man himself. In many cases, failures are nothing more than pathways to later success, simply because they can teach us more about ourselves and about God's nature than successes can. I believe that's because failures force us to stop and think about the decisions we've made.

Spiritually speaking, I've grown very little during the times when the skids are greased with the oil of gladness because of the blue sky I'm living under in the moment. But when the sled comes to a halt because the skids are dry and the heart is broken over current circumstances. . .it's during those seasons that God has my full attention.

Failures do not measure the man who gets up from the deck and presses forward. In fact, pressing on is exactly what God intends for us to do, because pressing on is the righteous action. It's spiritually "unnatural" for a man to go down and stay down. And when we rise up to face the future, we find God's greatest grace.

Perseverance—faithfully moving forward—is the stage where the journey is really meant to play out, for it's in the moving forward that we discover just how big this God of ours truly is.

RECONCILIATION

All this is from God, who reconciled us to himself through
Christ and gave us the ministry of reconciliation: that God
was reconciling the world to himself in Christ, not counting
people's sins against them. And he has committed
to us the message of reconciliation.
2 CORINTHIANS 5:18–19

Reconciliation. That's a tough word for many of us to hear—even tougher when someone has done us wrong.

When you are wronged, you feel the natural human emotion of anger, and that's not necessarily wrong. Even good Christians get angry, and there is not one thing wrong with that. The "wrong" comes when you give yourself permission to keep that anger inside your heart. You see, there's a big difference between getting angry and being an angry person.

People are people, and they're going to let you down or wrong you. That's just what happens when you live life on this side of heaven, where imperfect people act imperfectly.

That's why reconciliation is so crucial to your personal growth. When you refuse to reconcile, when you choose instead to dwell on wrongs done to you, it's you who ends up starving.

God has given you a new life through Christ. He has called you to be reconciled to Him, and He has also called you to carry on the message of reconciliation through the way you live every day.

Why reconcile? Because it's what people do when they know what it means to be forgiven themselves.

BARRIERS

There are many things I "live for," things that make life so sweet that I can't imagine doing without them. If I were forced to give up many of these things, the last one to go—the one I'd cling to with a white-knuckled grip—would be turkey hunting.

I know that in the bigger picture, turkey hunting is a small thing. I'd never choose to hear the sound of a gobble over the thundering voice of God, nor would I choose spending time among the dogwoods, hearing the sounds of singing birds while setting up on a tom, over spending time with my wife and sons.

I've learned so much about life, and the pursuit of Christ, during my springtime matches with the elusive feathered warrior. Not long ago, I was out with one of my soul brothers, Steve Chapman, filming a hunt. We ran up on a bird that is what I call a "Hollywood" bird—just dying to be on camera. The hunt would have been over five minutes after he flew down from his nightly roost, but it was about twenty minutes before Chap was able to pull the trigger. The cause for the extra fifteen minutes was a box wire fence. We didn't know it was there, but after we bagged the bird, we realized that he had been searching all that time for a way through the fence so he could get to a sweet, sexy, long-legged fantasy locked in his brain—which was actually me singing words of deception from a mouth call.

As we shot the posthunt segments, Steve and I determined that this gobbler's barrier, the fence, was actually his best friend. He spent fifteen minutes determined to find a way through and around it, but in the end he flew over that fence to get to what he wanted so badly. That fence, it turns

IT'S MORE LIKE A HEADLAMP, REALLY

I recently listened to a friend of mine preach a message centered around a verse that is familiar to us all: "Your word is a lamp for my feet, a light on my path" (Psalm 119:105).

He told me that quite often he'll ask his church, "Where are we going in our journey with God?"—and they respond, "We don't know!"

It's not that my brother was saying that followers of Christ should neglect planning. I know my preacher friend is on target with his theology because the truth of the matter is that we usually don't know where God is taking us. We can plan all we want, but God is the One directing our paths. After all, how many of you reading this now are in a job, a church, a relationship, or any life situation you never thought you'd be in today?

I can say "amen" to that. When I signed on with Jesus, I never dreamed I'd be doing what I'm doing today.

Never forget that being a Jesus follower means being a follower. We don't lead God. He leads us.

The older I get, the more I value planning well. A good plan has kept me on target in many life situations. However, I never want to mistake my love of planning for maturity when it's actually a form of insecurity that demonstrates itself in my fear of changing courses because I have no clue what a new one may bring.

My wife, Michelle, is a self-professed, high-octane control freak who values a secure daily plan. She taught me a great spiritual truth at a time in her life when she had no control whatsoever. I came home one day and she said, "You know, I've been reading Psalm 119. I crave security, but God has shown me that a lamp to my feet is not a spotlight shining miles down the road. It's a light to the path just ahead of my next step."

YOUR GREATEST FEAR

*"What good is it for someone to gain
the whole world, yet forfeit their soul?"*
MARK 8:36

The vast majority of men desire some level of worldly success. Whether it's financial success, the acquisition of more possessions, or simply the attainment of a position that brings him satisfaction, we men all want to have "achieved" something great.

Today, think about this question: What is it about success that truly motivates you?

A man's greatest fear should never be of failure, but rather of actually succeeding at something that doesn't really matter.

DRUMBEAT AND DIFFERENCES

Now you are the body of Christ, and each one of you is a part of it. And God has placed in the church first of all apostles, second prophets, third teachers, then miracles, then gifts of healing, of helping, of guidance, and of different kinds of tongues. Are all apostles? Are all prophets? Are all teachers? Do all work miracles? Do all have gifts of healing? Do all speak in tongues? Do all interpret? Now eagerly desire the greater gifts.

1 Corinthians 12:27–31

One of the greatest biblical truths I've learned about leadership is that great leaders have the ability to recognize, and even value, the differences in the people around them. The most difficult part of my leadership journey thus far has been taking so long to learn to value people who approach life, and their life's work, differently from me.

Paul is clear that God does not give every person every spiritual gift, and that's because God made us different from one another so that the body of Christ can be more effective. People with gifts of leadership (like me) are highly relational. We want to cast vision, encourage, motivate, communicate, teach, and, in a lot of cases, just enjoy dreaming about what God can do. We might even get around to putting those dreams down on paper.

What leaders need most is an administrator, someone who can actually execute a plan. People with gifts of administration are not so relational. They are rarely seen as "the life of the party," because they are too busy making sure there is plenty of food and drink.

Sometimes we tend to view people who see life differently from us as our adversaries. People with different gift sets operate in different ways, and sometimes it's difficult to make sense of it all. Through the years, though, I've actually learned to praise God for people He has wired so differently from the way He hardwired me.

Your life will be much easier, and your life's work will be much smoother, when you learn to see the glory of God in your teammates who stroll to the beat of a different drum.

Let me encourage you to take this even one step further. When it comes to dealing with a teammate, seek first to discover how he is wired. Is he a leader/visionary or an administrator/manager? Does he value the bottom line, or does he value mercy and compassion? Once you've discovered how your teammate thinks, the next time you have to work with him, think about how he is looking at this situation. You'll be amazed at how the people who once thought you were their adversary now understand that you're part of their team.

IMMOBILIZED BY BITTERNESS

See to it that no one falls short of the grace of God and
that no bitter root grows up to cause trouble and defile many.
HEBREWS 12:15

No person walking the planet is immune to anger. We all encounter it. It's just one of those unavoidable areas of life. Getting angry is one thing, but staying angry and allowing that anger to turn to bitterness is a whole different ball game.

You see, anger is a natural human emotion, but bitterness isn't, because bitterness is not of God.

I've often heard this saying, which is so true: "Harboring anger is like drinking poison and expecting someone else to get sick."

The thing about unresolved anger is that it is immobilizing. There will be times when you get angry. Just make sure the anger doesn't go unresolved. You can't afford it—it will immobilize your heart every time.

Now go back to the verse above and read it again. . .slowly. Notice the consequences of allowing bitterness to take hold within you. You'll never want to drink that poison again!

ONE BAD DAY

A servant girl saw [Peter] seated there in the firelight.
She looked closely at him and said, "This man was with him."
But he denied it. "Woman, I don't know him," he said.
LUKE 22:56–57

The older I get, the more I try to be slow in forming opinions—especially about people. I've learned that no matter what information I have about someone, and no matter how I got that information, I really can't know what factors in a person's life cause him to speak and behave the way he does.

I have caught myself making character assessments about a man off nothing more than one or two short encounters. But the truth of the matter is that there is no way one or two situational encounters can give me enough information to make an assessment about anyone.

What if that person was simply having a bad day—or a bad week, or month, or year? What if he was under a ton of stress in his marriage or in his job? It's a rare person who is completely "in character" during those seasons in life, and we do him no favors by assuming that the negativity he shows during that time reflects who he really is.

Let's talk about a bad day in the life of an important Bible character.

Other than Jesus Himself, the apostle Peter was the greatest New Testament preacher. Nobody, not even Paul, could get the kind of results Peter got when he preached to large crowds. But the funny thing is, if you ask most Christians to tell you one thing about Peter, they'll almost always bring up his denial of Christ.

MAKING COMPARISONS

*If anyone thinks they are something when they are not,
they deceive themselves. Each one should test their own
actions. Then they can take pride in themselves alone,
without comparing themselves to someone else,
for each one should carry their own load.*

GALATIANS 6:3–5

Though I'm a decent golfer, I'm smart enough to know better than to compare my game to that of a pro like Phil Mickelson. That would be stupid, and I try my best to avoid stupid, especially when it comes to comparing myself with others.

When it comes to golf (or anything else for that matter), I've noticed that I tend to compare myself to someone who lives and operates within my bracket of talent. . .or to someone who is far worse (at golf) than me.

The issue is not that it's bad that I want to compete. In fact, I believe that competition can be a good thing. The real issue is the danger in comparing myself to another person when it comes to my life in the faith. I can think of few things more deceptive and damaging to the soul than comparison, for comparison is never the best indicator of righteousness.

We should measure ourselves against one standard, and that is God and His standards. That means we need grace, and a lot of it.

We are all guilty of making comparisons between ourselves and others, and I believe I have a solution: just stop it!

My money, my talent, and my career trajectory are forever moving targets, but God's standards remain the same. God has never called me to compare myself to anyone but Him. He's called me to be obedient to Him, and it's in the obedience that success, the kind that lives beyond me, can be measured.

GOD THE CLOSER

The further along I go in my walk with Jesus, the more I see how God has designed things in such a way that each of us has our own position to play in the game of life.

In baseball, there are starting pitchers, who have a set of skills and a mentality geared toward the front end of the game. The starters usually give way to legendary, almost mythical human beings like Goose Gossage, Lee Smith, Mariano Rivera, or Bruce Sutter—whose skill sets and mentalities give them the intimidating fresh fire to finish the deal. It's a beautiful thing to see it work.

However, position contentment is not always as easy a concept to hone as it may seem. I see it even in the youth football team I coach, the Jets. At almost every practice, I tell the boys, "Only one or two of you is going to consistently get to tote the pigskin across the goal line. It takes every player, doing his job well, to make that happen." They haven't fully bought into this idea just yet, but I see progress in their nine-year-old minds.

It is usually no easier for adults to be content with playing a position. Many of us struggle with just playing a role, and playing it well, simply because our hearts so often strive for more. Which leads me to my point: God is the closer.

I am called to live my life in such a way that others can see God at work in me. I am called to live my life verbally too—by speaking freely of the way God is at work in me.

When it comes to how I relate to people, there's no biblical mandate, or Holy Spirit pressure, calling me to seal the eternal deal. And there is no savvy sales model to guide me in overcoming the theological objections of nonbelievers. My role is to sow the seed of God's Word by being a living witness who actively speaks and lives under the same covering of truth to which the blind man in John 9 testified: "One thing I do know. I was blind but now I see!" (verse 25).

That's my role: I sow, but God is the closer. What happens beyond the sowing is up to Him.

SEEING THE DIFFERENCE

Do not let your heart envy sinners,
but always be zealous for the fear of the Lord.
PROVERBS 23:17

I once had a conversation with an old friend in the faith who shared many miles and memories with me from my early days of salvation. We began to talk of the corporate nature of life and manhood—not in a negative way at all, because we both see value in what corporate leaders have to say about success and how to achieve various levels of it.

He made a very wise comment that day: "I see a lot of men, even pastors, who are reading, listening to, and even following corporate gurus, but I don't see many of the corporate gurus reading, listening to, or following what God has to say."

His words reminded me of something I've said many times. He and I were both in agreement that corporate wisdom from the Jim Collins and Stephen Covey types in this world can be amazingly helpful. Yet there are limits to the kind of influence they are to have on Jesus followers. The reason: corporate wisdom streams are not necessarily anointed with God's Holy Spirit. We do know, however, that God's Word is a guarantee for truth.

As men, we admire successful men. I'll be the first to admit that. Still, at the end of the day, I cannot allow my genuine admiration to take me to a place where I am overly influenced by sources that are not "washed in the blood." Why? Because corporate and cultural definitions of success and leadership are moving targets that change every few years, while God's definition of success never changes.

God's definition of success is measured by obedience to

His truths about life and how it should be lived, and those standards are not often mimicked, or even valued, in the corporate world.

We must be wise to the difference.

OUR GREAT ASSET

When it comes to career, most men work with and around a team of individuals. Knowing this, then, you can view the people with whom you work in two ways: you can see them as tools to be used to achieve organizational goals, or you can see people not as tools but as your greatest assets.

Sadly, the first option is by far the most common model around these days. Yet the second option seems better for turning organizations into healthy, vibrant operations.

When people feel as if they are genuinely valued for who they are and for what they bring to the team, they will elevate themselves and perform far better than they would under any business model designed only to enhance the corporate bottom line.

Kip Tindell, founder of the Container Store, said, "Milton Friedman said that the only reason a corporation exists is to maximize the return of the shareholder. Forget that. Do this instead: put the employee first, and that employee will take better care of the customer than anyone else."

If we Christians really believe that God created all people, and therefore that people matter most, then how could we ever choose to run, or help to run, a business or a church in any way contrary to that fundamental belief?

THE DISEASE OF CARNALITY

When people hear the word *carnality*, they often think of things like sexual immorality, extreme greed, gross demands for independence, or even grotesque social injustice. But those behaviors are just that: behaviors. They are *symptoms* of a carnal heart, and they can be compared to the symptoms of a virus-caused illness. Vomiting, headaches, and dizziness are not the problem for one suffering from an illness; the viral infection is the actual problem.

Carnality, which I would define as an attempt to find satisfaction or fulfillment outside of the heart of God, is a disease of the heart. Simply put, a carnal person is one who tries to do for himself what only God can do. Carnality is trying to accomplish supernatural living standards through human efforts and strength. And when a person attempts to live by one's own personal standards or one's own set of rules or one's own strength, life eventually breaks down and doesn't work.

You were never meant to do for yourself those things that only God can do.

PRAYING FOR SAFETY

I have been constantly on the move. I have been in danger from rivers, in danger from bandits, in danger from my fellow Jews, in danger from Gentiles; in danger in the city, in danger in the country, in danger at sea; and in danger from false believers.
2 CORINTHIANS 11:26

I often hear Christians praying for safety. I have a wife and two sons, and I don't want anything bad to happen to them, so I understand why people pray that way.

It seems as though many Christians are striving to be safe in all their endeavors. God gives us wisdom and common sense so that we won't live life in reckless abandon, but it seems to me that we overcompensate to the point that we fear any level of uncertainty or risk.

I don't know that I've ever heard a group of people who are about to go on a mission trip in the name of Jesus gather at a church meeting and pray something like, "God, take us anywhere You see fit and let us encounter any situation You see fit in order to bring awareness to Your great name."

A ship docked in a harbor is most certainly safe, but being tied up safely in a harbor is not the purpose for which the ship was created.

BLIND SIDES

If either of them falls down, one can help the other up.
But pity anyone who falls and has no one to help them up.
Also, if two lie down together, they will keep warm.
But how can one keep warm alone?
ECCLESIASTES 4:10–11

Men are a lot like bull elk in that we are typically emotional loners, except during the rut.

Then we seek companionship.

Over the years, I've learned that the biggest of the white-tails, elk, and virtually everything else with antlers have a tendency to be loners. The problem with being a loner is that it makes you vulnerable—*very* vulnerable.

Your personality may not be such that you need forty-three of your closest buddies around you all the time, but you cannot afford to be a loner. To ensure the survival of your heart, you must surround yourself with a few great men of God who can trek with you through the journey of manhood.

We all have blind sides, and that's where our enemy—the devil—likes to hit us the hardest. That's why we need other men around us, watching areas of our lives that we may well neglect if we live the life of a loner.

TOLERANCE

*Love does not delight in evil
but rejoices with the truth.*
1 CORINTHIANS 13:6

It seems that every day we hear pop culture and other media sources singing the praises of tolerance. Tolerance is no longer just a virtue; it is now a commandment. For without tolerance, we're told, we cannot be in the righteous flock of God's "loving people."

The problem is that the popular definition of the word *tolerance* has changed. Tolerance actually means living in harmony with people—especially people who engage in thinking or lifestyles with which you don't agree. However, that's not what it means in today's culture. Today's brand of tolerance demands that you not only embrace other lifestyles and thinking, but fully endorse them—lest you be labeled as bigoted, backward, mean-spirited, or even anti-intellectual. Now, tolerance is seen as a rite of passage for those who want to be seen as "good" people with righteous hearts.

Tolerance may be politically correct, but it will never be biblically correct. The reason is simple: God will never call you to be tolerant of anything His Son had to die for in order to forgive.

Love and tolerance are not the same thing. Grace is of the Lord; tolerance is not. Grace is based on God's holy love; tolerance is based on deception.

God never called you to be a religious jerk or to be arrogant about your convictions. He has, however, called you to live a life of righteousness, and to live that life out loud.

NOBODY TO BLAME

"Neither this man nor his parents sinned," said Jesus, "but this happened so that the works of God might be displayed in him."
JOHN 9:3

It's a story often overlooked in the grand drama of all that Jesus did for humanity. Like every documented story we have of Jesus' life, this story holds a profound truth within it. Yet it's like driving through a small town with no stoplight. . . blink and you'll miss it.

Jesus encountered a blind man, and His crew asked Him, "Rabbi, who sinned, this man or his parents, that he was born blind?"

Jesus' answer stunned the disciples, for they were used to thinking that bad fortune was always the result of someone's wrongdoing. "Neither this man nor his parents sinned," He said.

So what happened to this fella? Answer: life happened. Who knows why he was born blind. But that wasn't the real issue. The issue that mattered most was that Jesus found a way for this man's set of challenges to glorify God.

Life—good life, bad life, and in-between life—happens to all of us. It's all life.

How is the glory of God going to be displayed in your life—as life of all kinds comes your way?

IDENTITY

*What do people get for all the toil and anxious striving with which
they labor under the sun? All their days their work is grief and pain;
even at night their minds do not rest. This too is meaningless.*

ECCLESIASTES 2:22–23

It's the thing that defines who you are, the answer you give to let others know who you are. When you meet someone for the first time, one of the first things you are asked is, "What do you do?"

We men tend to get a major part of our sense of self-worth from what we do for a living. Our careers define us—or at least where our careers take us defines us.

So we put in long hours and work with relentless pursuit. And for what?

The CEO of a Fortune 500 company and a homeless beggar on the street have something in common—namely, they both have a date with death. And on that day, both men will stand naked before God.

Who do you think really wins on that day—the CEO because he had a liquid net worth and lived large, or the beggar because he made it through life with nothing and took nothing with him when he left this earth?

I wouldn't want to be a beggar, but I wouldn't want to be the CEO of a Fortune 500 company, either. Having a great work ethic is admirable, but obsession with your career is not. There is one thing I do know that I don't want, and that's to work my life away only to realize in the end that I neglected life itself and the people around me.

My identity comes from having the power of Holy God residing in me. Paul said that "Christ in you" is the hope of glory. If I gain my sense of self from that, then eternal paradise is my destiny.

SOVEREIGN INTERRUPTIONS

Highways in most every major American city have HOV lanes. These lanes were created for commuters with passengers in their vehicles so they can travel faster than the crowd in the other lanes.

The HOV lane certainly reflects our culture. We live in a microwave culture. We want everything, and we want it *now*. No person is exempt from this constant pressure to "get moving." We've almost come to a point where any form of delay causes immediate frustration.

Just recently, I was traveling in the mountains of eastern Kentucky. They have no HOV lane there. You're doing well if there is a road that leads to where you want to go!

Off the beaten path, tucked away in a small home surrounded by Kentucky hardwood hills, I met an old preacher. We talked for what must have been an hour. I had some filming to do, some projects to complete before the next day. Yet God's Spirit kept telling me, *"Don't rush this."*

Nothing profound necessarily came from the encounter, except that I knew I was talking with a man who walked with God. And those are the men you need to spend time with.

In today's world, interruptions are often viewed as harsh, unwelcome, unwanted breaks into our daily schedule. I'm convinced that many of these disturbances in our days are sovereign interruptions our holy God designed beforehand . . .for our benefit.

EIGHT PEOPLE

There are many areas in life that we neglect out of the simple assumption that somebody else is on top of it. Take politics for instance. Our nation's representatives have no real idea of accountability because we as citizens don't hold them accountable. We always assume somebody is on top of things, when in fact it's our very own job that we are neglecting.

Believe it or not, the same is true with the concept of encouragement.

Did you know that studies have shown that the average pastor will resign and walk away from a church over. . .wait for it. . .eight people? Just eight people make his life so miserable that he gives up. Even in churches that host thousands of people in worship, the average pastor is not exempt from the influence of eight people who seek to destroy his spirit.

If you were the devil, how would you go about destroying the spirit of a man of God? Would you cause him grief by having the city council sue him for preaching the Gospel? If I were the devil, I know exactly how I'd destroy a pastor's spirit. I'd put eight of the most sour, bitter people front and center on Sunday morning so that when he preaches he must look at their "faithful" faces. I'd find a way to make them deacons and committee members so that he must deal with their venom at every turn.

Pastors face incredible spiritual battles, but the average church member never knows it until the battle has gone public and the pastor is already on his way out the door. In a church of 500 members, what would happen if the voices of the "great eight" fell on deaf ears because the pastor was surrounded by 492 ambassadors of encouragement?

Don't worry about it, though; somebody else is on top of it.

INTO THE LIGHT IN A MATTER OF SECONDS

Even the darkness will not be dark to you; the night
will shine like the day, for darkness is as light to you.
PSALM 139:12

Some time ago, I hopped on an airplane to travel to a church to speak. No matter how many times I've done it before, I still cannot look out of the window of an airplane without being immediately reminded of the sovereignty of God. Perhaps it's my simplicity of mind, but I am always amazed at how I can leave the tarmac in a rainy, cloudy mess, only to be looking at cloudless blue sky as soon as the plane beats its way through the storm cover.

Each time that happens, I feel the power of God and His Spirit reminding me that darkness does not affect Him. No storm rattles Him, and no rain washes away His ability to see things as they truly are.

When you are struggling through a storm, when you feel the engines of your soul working hard to pull out of it, simply remember your God. He is the same God Moses asked for guidance when he could find none anywhere else. He is the same God who guided Joshua step by little step to the Promised Land. And He is the same God who gave Paul a reason to elevate his mind to worship while his career seemed literally shipwrecked on an island.

To our God, there is no darkness, because He is light . . .and His light illuminates life for us to see it the way He means for it to be seen.

NO MATTER WHAT

"A tithe of everything from the land,
whether grain from the soil or fruit from the trees,
belongs to the Lord; it is holy to the Lord."
LEVITICUS 27:30

Tough financial times can squeeze a man. But the great thing about our God is that He never changes. He's rock solid, and so are His commandments. So when times get tough, you must make a decision—do you believe God for who He says He is, or do you not?

Our most recent recession will not be the last time the economy will get bad. The economy changes like the wind, but God's commandments calling us to be financially faithful do not.

How can a man have the guts to ask God to bless him with a great job and stable income while at the same time willfully disobeying the very God he is praying to by neglecting to bring Him the tithe?

You are the spiritual leader of your home, so be the man. Make a decision that no matter how depleted the bank account becomes, you will choose to honor God with your tithe. You just may find that your decision to be financially faithful is the only thing that brings you out of a financial storm.

LET YOUR FOCUS FIT YOUR DESIGN

*Blessed is the one. . .whose delight is in the law of
the LORD, and who meditates on his law day and night.*
PSALM 1:1–2

The biblical meaning of the word *meditation* is often misunderstood. The word *meditate* as it is used in Psalm 1:2 does not imply that you must walk around in a Zen-like, "ohm" state of mind. On the contrary, the Hebrew meaning of this word is simply "focus."

Focus is critical, yet not all great men of God do it the same way. Some men get up early, even before dawn, to talk with God. However, others find they do not have the ability to focus well or get the most out of their time with God that early.

One of the greatest freedoms I've enjoyed in my walk with Christ is that of giving myself permission to be creative with my personal devotions, especially when it comes to prayer. I began to focus on praying all day long—short prayers, long prayers. . .it really doesn't matter. What matters is that I take the time to talk with the Lord more than just in those few minutes in the morning when I have a devotion time.

There's a phrase in Christianity that you'll hear in reference to someone's spiritual life: their "walk with God." Walking implies action. It is dynamic, not static. Let your walk fit your personality. Just be sure you have the focus. . .to stay focused.

VIOLATING EVERYTHING
HE KNOWS TO BE TRUE

For the lips of the adulterous woman drip honey, and her speech is smoother than oil; but in the end she is bitter as gall, sharp as a double-edged sword. Her feet go down to death; her steps lead straight to the grave.

PROVERBS 5:3–5

You may not be a hunter, but you can learn a simple truth from the wild turkey that just might keep you from suffering the death of all you hold sacred.

A tom is the ultimate male stud. When he goes into strut and displays his strength and dominance, the ladies just can't resist. They often break into a flat-out run to get to him before any competitors come calling. In fact, the tom's created nature dictates that he stay put while the hens do the work to get to him. He never chases the females; they always come to him.

Almost always, that is.

On occasion a tom will hear an elusive hen. She's sexy in the way she talks to him, and she is long legged and mysterious. She just moves differently than the rest of the girls.

Then the tom does something that violates his nature. He will actually investigate her just a bit. He'll move closer, but she walks even farther from him. He can't see every part of her, yet he can't help but visualize what she must look like when the light hits her late in the evening. She's supposed to come to him, and he knows it.

They keep talking, and he goes against everything he knows to be true and moves closer. Sweet sounds fill the air. . .right up until he hears the boom of a shotgun blast leading to his death.

The sweet voice that tom heard wasn't a hen at all; it was his adversary, giving him exactly what he wanted until he had him in gun range. I've looked down my gun barrel countless times as I watched a tom lose his life simply because he violated the truths that had kept him alive in a hostile world.

BEN HOGAN AND BALANCE

*For just as each of us has one body with many members,
and these members do not all have the same function,
so in Christ we, though many, form one body, and each
member belongs to all the others. We have different gifts,
according to the grace given to each of us.*

ROMANS 12:4–6

The late Ben Hogan was one of the greatest golfers ever to play the game. To this day, golf gurus proclaim that he may have been the best ball striker of all time. He did, however, struggle with his putter at times.

Hogan, a winner of four US Opens, two Masters, two PGA Championships, and a British Open, once told the golfing world a little secret: he hated the eleventh green at Augusta National, home of the Masters. He said the green was far too complex to putt on consistently, so he intentionally missed it every time, just slightly to the right of the putting surface. He would then chip up close, make his par putt, and move on. Hogan knew exactly how to play to his strengths, and that is what made him Ben Hogan.

God has given you specific spiritual gifts. They came into your life at the same time the Holy Spirit entered your heart. God did not give you every gift there is, but He did give you some specific gifts that shape who you are in Christ.

Balance is a myth. No person is balanced when it comes to the areas of his strength. Reggie McNeal, author of *Get a Life! It is All about You*, says, "Your gifts are the places where you are out of round."

The problem is that far too often, we seek to improve on our weaknesses only to let our strengths suffer. God wants you to serve Him, and your best shot at making an impact in this world is to play from a position of the gifts God has given you.

Feeling burned out in ministry? Check to see if you are serving through your strengths. You may find that you were never meant to be in the role you're in to begin with.

LAW OF THE HARVEST

A man reaps what he sows. Whoever sows to please their flesh,
from the flesh will reap destruction; whoever sows to please
the Spirit, from the Spirit will reap eternal life.
GALATIANS 6:7–8

There is a law at work in the universe that no man made:
the law of the harvest. Holy God set it into motion.

People have tried to reinvent it over the years, diluting
it down to catchy phrases like "karma" or "what goes around
comes around." But it's much deeper than that.

The law of the harvest is demonstrated in every area of
a man's life. A man reaps what he sows in his business life—
in every contract, every networking relationship, and every
investment. A man reaps what he sows with his family—his
time, his attitude, and his ability to show love. There's no
part of life where a man can escape this divine law.

Found within the law of the harvest is a promise from
God to claim. Because of God's reconciling nature, no matter how poorly a man has sown in his past, God brings a new
field and a new plow, complete with new seed to be sown.

It's because of His deep desire for reconciliation that
God chooses to give us the promise that poor sowing choices
of our past don't have to mean a poor harvest in our future.

Every day God offers a man yet another chance to sow
seeds of righteousness that yield fresh crops for the days
ahead. It's simply a matter of how you choose to plant your
life and sow your influence.

A SUBTLE DECEPTION

A while back, I began scheduling out my days two weeks at a time. I know it sounds like a stupid, even slightly comical, exercise in futility. . .except that it's working.

I've read how successful people commonly lay out their goals and then plan weeks in advance for the daily progress toward those goals. My justification for not doing it was always found somewhere in the idea that "I'm just not built that way."

We all have different personalities, and I knew better than to compare my own operational prowess to that of other men. But I knew I needed to lay out plans for achieving my goals. Actually having a plan *became* the goal for me.

So I decided to try it. I carved out a ninety-day plan for what I wanted to accomplish, and then I broke that plan down day by day, appointment by appointment.

Let me tell you: a mere six days into the experiment, I was depressed—depressed over how my lazy nature had kept me from doing this fifteen years ago. For you see, six days into this journey, I felt as if I'd accomplished more in that single week than I had done in a long, long time before that. For the first time in a long time, what was actually important won out over what was urgent. I wasn't just spending the day putting out fires; I was steadily moving the ball down the field.

Then it happened. Around day ten into this venture, I was so caught up in the elation of knocking out my punch list for all matters crucial to the kingdom of God that I didn't keep my 6:00 a.m. appointment with my Father (the heavenly One).

He wasn't disappointed, for He doesn't measure His love

for me based on my pursuits. Still, though, He did speak to me about it. Late that night He spoke to me, reminding me never to believe the sweet, sweet lie that working for Him is as important as being with Him. He reminded me never to mistake activity for progress.

PASSION AND KNOWLEDGE

When you put two different translations of Proverbs 19:2 side by side, you gain quite an interesting perspective on life, passion, and mistakes made. Just take a look:

- "Also it is not good for a person to be without knowledge, and he who hurries his footsteps errs" (NASB).
- "Enthusiasm without knowledge is no good; haste makes mistakes" (NLT).

The word *zeal* can be defined as passion for a cause. And passion for a cause without the knowledge of how to carry out that cause is something I know a lot about. Sometime around 1999 God began to give me a vision for reaching hunters with the Gospel and for empowering Jesus-following hunters to use their passion for God in harmony with their passion for the outdoors. The problem was, I didn't have a clue how to go about doing it.

Passion is mission critical to a life that counts, but when you have no knowledge to accompany your passion, you spend your zealous energy recklessly and make mistakes. To employ some hunting terminology, you take a shotgun approach to life rather than a rifle approach. That's what I so often did.

What I've found over the years is that "enthusiasm without knowledge" translates into a lot of money wasted, relationships strained, and dreams drained. Passion for a cause can cause you to shoot first and aim later.

Shotguns certainly have their place, but they're not nearly as good as rifles when you're aiming at a specific target.

IN THE ZONE

That person is like a tree planted by streams of water,
which yields its fruit in season and whose leaf does
not wither—whatever they do prospers.
PSALM 1:3

Great athletes often refer to the state of mind that allows them to perform at their very best as "the zone."

There's no denying that a zone exists, for we catch glimpses of it in every sport. We've seen great athletes such as Joe Montana, Larry Bird, Michael Jordan, Jack Nicklaus, Tiger Woods, Tom Brady, and Nolan Ryan elevate their games above those of other great athletes and accomplish things that leave us speechless.

Great men of God experience life in a unique position, but be keenly aware of this truth: a man can't arrive in "the zone" of God's favor through hard work and sheer talent alone. The only reason the person mentioned in the verse above is blessed is because he has taken a position near the living water. He is blessed because the roots of his heart go deep and stay planted in the stream of God's life-giving Spirit. It's the water flowing into him that creates "the zone."

If you want to be in "the zone" in your walk with God, you have to remember that positioning is everything.

MAKING ACQUISITIONS

Get wisdom, get understanding.
Proverbs 4:5

Men are built to gain ground. Dominance is within our created design. We are naturally seekers of control. God isn't necessarily against that; in fact, He made us the way we are. He just wants us to make sure we're working to gain the right things.

We men so often spend our lives battling for better careers, better homes, better gear, better networks, better educations, and better financial stability. There's nothing wrong with that—unless we let the most precious acquisitions elude us as we chase the material glitter, the things that will prove themselves inconsequential in helping us finish the race of life as winners in the eyes of God.

The Word of God tells us to get wisdom. A man can spend his entire life acquiring the inconsequential, only to find he's a fool in the end because he doesn't possess the wisdom of God.

THE POWER OF PERMISSION

For this reason I remind you to fan into flame the gift of God,
which is in you through the laying on of my hands.
2 Timothy 1:6

Over the years in ministry, I've discovered an odd truth I have seen play out in my life over and over again. I cannot explain it, but I know it's true, for I've seen it play out too many times to deny it. That truth is this: people sometimes need permission to be who God created them to be.

You are not God, and neither am I. But as Jesus followers, we are people God uses to do His speaking.

I don't believe the "gift" Paul wrote of in the verse above actually came into Timothy's being just because Paul physically touched him, thus giving Timothy the gift of preaching. Paul was a mere mortal, and that fact alone disqualifies him from being the gift giver. Only the Spirit of God can inject gifts into a person.

In his first letter to Timothy, Paul makes many references indicating that he and other men in Timothy's life had been given prophecies or visions revealing that God had given Timothy the spiritual gift of preaching, and thus they "bestowed" that gift on him. They were in effect saying, "Timothy, we all see that you are called to preach, and we want to lay hands on you and pray over you to confirm it."

You should never say certain things about a man's future just because you feel spiritual at the moment. However, when you see a gift of God active in someone, open your mouth and tell him what you see. Tell him his gift has blessed you and helped move you forward in the faith—and be specific when you do it. It may be that God wants to use you to set this person free to serve God by letting him know that God has given him a specific spiritual gift.

The best I can tell, God has given me three spiritual gifts mentioned in the scriptures. Early on in my ministry, I had no idea I had two of those gifts. But at various times in my early years of ministry, people would tell me how God had used those gifts to move them on in the faith. After hearing that feedback so many times, I began searching deeper into what the Bible says about those gifts, only to realize they had been there all along. All it took for me to feel the freedom to begin operating in those gifts consistently was to have people in the body of Christ confirm that God had given them to me.

INFORMATION OVERLOAD

*For there is one God and one mediator between
God and mankind, the man Christ Jesus.*
1 Timothy 2:5

There has never been a time in human history when information was as easily accessible as it is today. I don't know about you, but there are times when all this access actually works against me.

I've noticed that if I'm not careful, this information overload can bog down my decision making. That's because I can go online and find a thousand positive reviews and a thousand negative reviews—any of which can validate any decision I want to make—on any gadget, vehicle, book, or vacation rental.

I suppose this is one of the reasons the simplicity of God is such a beacon to my soul. In a world of Google searches, social media, and access to information that is often more confusing than helpful, God has, since the dawn of time, made Himself easy to find.

God's message to me is clear: there is one God and only one way to get to Him—through His Son.

NO SUBSTITUTE FOR START

Go to the ant, you sluggard; consider its ways and be wise!
It has no commander, no overseer or ruler, yet it stores
its provisions in summer and gathers its food at harvest.
PROVERBS 6:6–8

The ant doesn't need anyone looking over its thorax telling it to get to work. The ant is the ultimate example of what we today call a "self-starter."

Whether it's on Twitter, through an email, or when I'm speaking at a live event, about once a week someone asks me, "How did you get into writing books, speaking, and the other things you do?"

I could answer that question by talking about the many things that have fueled my efforts since day one, but it all goes back to this: I started.

You can research all you want. Think over something all you want. Strategize all you want. Even talk with experts all you want. But there never has been, nor will there ever be, any substitute for actually getting up and moving toward the calling God has on your life. To put it in one simple word: Start!

SCREAMING WHEAT

Imagine if you were to walk up to a farmer and tell him you want to make money off a crop of wheat, but you don't want to plant it. That farmer buddy of yours would laugh you off the front porch, put his hand on your shoulder as you walked back to your vehicle, and find a down-home, witty way—as so many farmers can do—to tell you that you need to get some *common sense*.

I recently went on a mission trip to Moldova. As we traveled to the orphan camp, I noticed something. Each day we'd turn right off a paved road onto a dirt road. As we traveled down the dirt road, which was about a half mile long, I realized we never left a wheat field. God was silently screaming to me through His creation. It occurred to me that the only road leading to the place where we were going to both be and share the Gospel was lined by a crop.

Evangelicals love working in the harvest, but you cannot reap what hasn't been sown. Someone must sow the truth of the Gospel of Christ by sowing the love found in it.

Before you share words about your Jesus, do not offend people's common sense by neglecting to sow His love into their lives. The season of harvest never comes before the season of planting.

IMAGINE IF YOU COULD. . .

Imagine, if you can, the possibility that you could earn God's favor. Imagine what that would look like.

Imagine the hectic pace at which you'd live trying to chase the standard.

Imagine the mental torture that would plague you every night as you would try to sleep yet could not, as thoughts of wondering if you made the grade with everything you did today kept you awake.

Imagine how complicated your life would become over time as you constantly compared yourself with those you believed were living righteously (or unrighteously), never realizing that you had no clue who they really were behind closed doors.

Do you really want God to love you based on how you act?

Do you really want God to love you based on where you stand morally, relative to the vast majority of people?

Do you really want God to love you based on *all* the thoughts that run through your head?

God is perfect, and in His perfection, He knew better than to give you a key performance indicator (KPI) for daily life, for if life did consist of Yahweh's KPIs, humanity wouldn't last a decade without self-destructing.

In His perfection, God gave you an open invitation to come in from out of the rain. He gave you a pass on a test you'd never be prepared to take.

In His perfection, He gave you Jesus, who said, "Come to me, all of you who are weary and carry heavy burdens, and I will give you rest" (Matthew 11:28 NLT).

KEEPING YOUR DISTANCE

Keep to a path far from her.
PROVERBS 5:8

Men are taught that we can handle situations. No man wants to think anyone or anything is stronger than he is.

Solomon tells us that there are things, situations, and even people we simply shouldn't go near. Here's the reason: once a man plays with fire and doesn't get burned, he will play with it again. Not only that, he'll find that the rush of being in no-man's-land and then walking away gives him a false sense of security.

Yet you and I both know his day is coming.

Strength is found in knowing that all it's taken to build your life up to this point is far too precious to risk. Keep your distance from the adulteress. . .and from anything that even dimly bears her reflection.

THE POWER OF SIN

*Lest you lose your honor to others
and your dignity to one who is cruel.*
PROVERBS 5:9

In a very real way, the power of sin deserves admiration. What causes me awe, what makes me respect (and fear) sin's power even more than the destruction it causes is the lingering effect it has on a man once the walls come down and his downfall is made known.

After Hurricane Katrina hit the Gulf Coast, I went to Mississippi with several men. We gathered chain saws and started clearing downed trees for people whose lives had been devastated as tornadoes ripped through their state.

What stunned me the most about what I saw on that trip was that though Katrina ripped through Mississippi in a matter of a few hours, her wrath was felt for years to come among those trying to recover from the damage. Some people evacuated before the storm hit and never came back. Their homes and their communities were in ruins, and they simply started over. . .somewhere far from an ocean.

That's much like the awe-inspiring power of sin, isn't it? It's not how hard it can make the wind blow and beat against your life, and it's not how fiercely its bite can be felt. It's the width and depth of the wounds it leaves—wounds that can take years to heal.

Do not give your years to one who is cruel.

A GENTLE ANSWER

A gentle answer turns away wrath.
PROVERBS 15:1

One night when my son Tucker was three years old, I sat at our kitchen table answering some emails. I couldn't see him, but I knew from the sounds coming from behind me that Tucker was getting into the pantry.

Even before Tuck was born, I had a sneaking suspicion (or maybe it was a warning from the Holy Ghost) that he'd have more than a nominal dose of grit.

He had been instructed twice to stay out of the pantry. So at this point, he was about to own a spanking.

"Tucker, are you supposed to be in that pantry?" I said.

"No, sir," he answered back. However, his brain wasn't communicating with his feet, for in the pantry he stayed, not willing to give up titled ground.

I launched into a fit of parental frustration that included a thirty-second diatribe about the importance of making good decisions that went something like this: "Tucker, right now is the moment you must make a decision. If you get a spanking, it's because you chose it. Right now you must make a decision whether or not to obey. Either way, it's your decision."

Long. . .deafening. . .silence.

"Tucker, I want to know right now. What's your decision?"

"Well, Dad, I've made a decision. . .that I love you."

I can't remember what happened after that. I'm guessing my laughter covered the transgression.

ONE WORD THAT CHANGES YOUR STORY FOREVER

My son, if you accept my words. . .
PROVERBS 2:1

I'm a grown man, and I no longer have to finish my dinner in order to eat dessert. I can eat my dessert and then eat dinner if I want to. In fact, I can eat two desserts and walk away from the feast happier than if I had eaten any dinner at all. I can walk into my doctor's office for my annual physical, and when he tells me my cholesterol is out of whack, I can keep on moving down the road of life any way I choose.

The truth is, I can do whatever I want. However, there are no free lunches, and when I don't listen to sound counsel, there are consequences. I can hear the truth, but hearing the truth and receiving the truth are not the same thing.

The word in the above verse that will change your story forever is "if."

If you read this verse as most people do, you will likely go right past the opening line, which sets the tone for everything that follows. *"If you accept my words. . . ,"* as in, "Hey, I'm not forcing you to do anything, but if you'll listen. . ."

The older I get, the more I realize that where I am is where I want to be, and where I want to be is nothing more than a series of choices I make to get there. I make those choices one at a time, and I make them based on whether I decide to use wisdom in the moment.

Hearing and receiving are two different things entirely. If we're wise, we'll listen to God—and those He places in our lives—when it's time to make a decision.

THE UGLIEST MAN I'VE EVER SEEN

I've seen some ugly men in my life.

I remember standing about four people back from a fella in line at a Taco Bell one day. I stood there watching and, regretfully, listening as he got plain nasty, yelling curse words because a woman working at the counter took too long to fill his ten-year-old son's order.

That dad was ugly, but he wasn't the ugliest man I have ever seen.

I remember sitting in class one Tuesday morning when a theologically renowned seminary professor brutally embarrassed a student for simply raising his hand to ask a question. The student didn't know that the theologian had an unspoken rule requiring students to ask their questions in the last sixty seconds of the lecture. This professor felt the student's inability to read his professorial mind gave him a license to go on a loud, childish rant about what he saw as the student's insensitivity. That was really ugly.

Then there was the time I stood among a group of men at a trade show as a legend in the hunting industry standing there with us made a pass at a woman who was a sales rep for a gun company. It was pathetic. And ugly.

Looking back on it, though, I think the prize for the ugliest man I have ever seen actually goes to. . .me. I have demonstrated my ugly side far too many times to count, and that ugliness comes from the nastiest trait residing in my soul: selfishness.

My selfishness has caused more pain than I care to remember. When I take a look inside myself, I can think of no sin I've committed that isn't born from the simplicity of selfishness. Far too many times, I have put my own desires, or my need to be seen, counted, known, or included, in front of other people. I have put myself first too many times. And it is always ugly.

I often pray that one day I can get past my selfishness, and yet I am often reminded that no foulmouthed fella at Taco Bell, no egotistical seminary professor, and no lust-filled hunting legend has anything on me when it comes to what goes on inside my selfish self.

AN IDEA IN JEOPARDY

I'm not exactly sure how a nation's core values get lost, but I suppose there are countless ways in which we lose touch with the bedrock beliefs that make up our worldview.

I do know, however, that too often we take our core values as Americans for granted. We hear a word like "freedom," but most of us have never been held captive at the end of another man's gun. We grin when someone speaks a word like "patriot," yet most of us will never know what it's like to sleep, soaking wet, under a blanket on a battlefield.

It was not difficult to tell that President Reagan struggled as he finished his speech on Memorial Day, May 28, 1984, as he spoke directly to the Unknown Soldier being laid to rest. In words from the heart of a father who actually believed in the idea of a great America, President Reagan called him "Dear son."

Our core values get lost when dads fail to explain to their sons and daughters why America is called "the land of the free and the home of the brave." We must tell our sons and daughters the story, or what's left of our values will surely be gone forever within a few generations.

I took Cole to the Veterans Cemetery one Memorial Day. It's a beautiful, solemn place in the hills of middle Tennessee. Standing in view of the white crosses that clad the cemetery, I told him that he gets to play baseball because he is free, that he gets to own a gun and go hunting because men before him died to defend his rights. I will tell him that the idea of freedom is just that—an idea—and I will tell him that ideas can be stolen and replaced unless we remember that there are truths worth dying for, and that the men buried before him did that very thing so that one day a little boy could live a life they never got to finish.

UNCOMMON DILIGENCE

The lazy do not roast any game,
but the diligent feed on the riches of the hunt.
PROVERBS 12:27

There are some truths that just stick inside your bones, never to leave again. They guide your thinking from the moment you first encounter them. Such was the case the first time I read President Calvin Coolidge's statement, "Nothing is more common than unsuccessful men with talent."

Those words were posted on the wall in my high school biology class, and they have penetrated my marrow ever since.

Intelligence was never my gift. I suppose if you added up my lifetime GPA, it would be 3.0 at best. People think I'm joking, but I'm not, when I say, "I'm living proof you can earn a doctorate on extra credit."

Talent is everywhere. At every turn, stage, and season in life, I've encountered stunningly talented people living hauntingly boring lives.

The diligent feed on the riches of the hunt not because they are better hunters, but because they are men who have learned one thing: a man who refuses to quit is incredibly hard to beat.

WHEN CLEAR LINES GO FOGGY

The older I get, the more I realize I'm never going to have everything I think I need.

Let me say at the outset, I'm not coming at this from a standpoint of materialism or greed that drives me to fill an insatiable appetite for more. What I mean is this: in life, there are *needs* and there are *wants*.

What the enemy does, however, is so badly blur the line between what we truly need and what we merely want that we start believing that our lives will be stable only once we have those things we only *think* we need.

When Jesus told us to "seek first the kingdom of God," He was in the middle of a discussion about anxiety, worry, and stability.

I'm learning that I can't live the life I don't have. I can only be faithful to the life I have now. And what I have, right now, is what God means for me to have today.

And that's enough.

DRIVEN DEEP

May the Lord direct your hearts
into God's love and Christ's perseverance.
2 THESSALONIANS 3:5

A personal trainer once challenged me to write down every single thing I ate over a seven-day period. I took him up on the challenge, and I learned something about myself: I had been living in complete oblivion when it came to the caliber of my nutritional life.

Since that time, I've asked myself, "What if I were to take the time to audit the subjects over which I tend to pray?" I'm sure the results would be very revealing.

The apostle Paul had some deep friends in the faith, and he prayed for them regularly. But he didn't pray so much that God would meet all their physical needs as that He would give them what they needed most: a deeper understanding of His love.

Here's what I've learned about God's love for me: He has no performance standard when it comes to His love. His love for me isn't based on what I can do for Him, or on what I can do in His name.

The more I wrap my mind around the simple truth that God's love for me has no driving force other than the love itself, the more I understand that I truly have everything I need.

When I lose sight of the truth that my heavenly Father's love isn't driven by performance standards, then I begin traveling down the wrong paths as I search for significance. When I hold tightly to God's love for me, my grip on the lesser things that surround me loosens.

WRESTLING A MEAN DOG

*Like one who grabs a stray dog by the ears is
someone who rushes into a quarrel not their own.*
PROVERBS 26:17

The imagery of the above verse always makes me think of my grandfather. This was his kind of wisdom—funny, yet forever true. After all, who in his right mind would walk up to a stray dog and grab it by the ears? The very thought of it makes me laugh a little.

When I was a kid, I would go into country stores that had game rooms in the back. Most of these rooms included a flipperless pinball machine that would pay out earnings—but more often than not, it was the pinball machine doing the earning. My grandfather, Josh Cruise, said of feeding those machines your hard-earned money: "Anything that backs its hind end up to a wall and challenges the whole world should be left alone."

Some things just need to be left alone. That can include some of the situations that surround you as you move through the marketplace of business. The key is knowing when to move in and when to walk on by.

I'm learning that there are situations that simply do not warrant my presence or my attention. I cannot tell you how many times my life has remained peaceful because I stopped and said to myself, "God hasn't called *me* to fix *that*."

UPSIDE-DOWN WISDOM

Humility is the fear of the LORD;
its wages are riches and honor and life.
PROVERBS 22:4

Almost every chapter in the book of Proverbs contains some sort of warning against arrogance, pride, or a stubborn heart. The simple truth is that a proud man is a man in danger—*real* danger.

The irony of that truth is that from the earliest days of childhood, we have it drilled into our hearts that we should take pride in ourselves and in our work. Pride is how life is supposed to work in the marketplace. Pride is supposed to drive a man's work ethic. Pride is what pushes a man to live and perform to high standards.

When you run that kind of thinking against the standard God has revealed in His written Word, you'll see that it's just the upside-down wisdom of a dying world. The Bible teaches us that humility, not pride, is at the heart of what we need to achieve success as God has defined it.

Riches, honor, and life—a trifecta that pop culture says comes from the hard work of a self-made man. Yet true riches, bestowed honor, and lasting life are not the result of human pride but of the fear of a God who has promised to bless those who humbly rely on Him.

WATER AND WORLDLY PURSUITS

"Everyone who drinks this water will be
thirsty again, but whoever drinks the water
I give them will never thirst. Indeed,
the water I give them will become in them
a spring of water welling up to eternal life."
JOHN 4:13-14

There are many things in life that are neither good nor bad—they just are. To borrow a commonly used pop culture phrase, "It is what it is."

That's the sort of path my mind takes when I read of Jesus' encounter with the woman at the well in John 4. She's looking for water and Jesus tells her that there is, in fact, water in this well. There's nothing inherently bad about the water. It's just that the water she's going to get from the bottom of that hole won't fulfill her greatest need.

A man looks for hope in a career like wealth management because he believes that he can make some money and have some level of financial security. Another man looks for a sense of identity in his career because he believes a meaningful career can be his contribution to the world around him. Yet another man looks for a relationship because he believes he will find the meaning of life in loving and being loved.

None of these things are wrong in and of themselves. Nothing wrong with wanting financial security. Nothing wrong with wanting a career that means something. Nothing wrong with loving and being loved. In fact, each can provide some level of soul satisfaction. The problem is, every man who looks for ultimate meaning in them will be thirsty again, simply because earthly pursuits can only yield earthly rewards.

Then there's this thing called living water, which comes with a promise: drink this and it'll put every other thing in perspective, because once you taste the difference, you can't go back to just getting water from a hole.

PRONE TO WANDER

The grace of the Lord Jesus be with you.
1 CORINTHIANS 16:23

I blew it.

Dropped the ball.

Made a blunder.

Messed up.

Fouled up.

The metaphors describing ways we sin seem endless.

It's no secret that we live in a fallen world. Every day we are confronted with the simple reality that brokenness is everywhere. No person is immune to it, for we are all touched in some way by the realities of sin.

Since we are all bound together in this earthly journey, the next time you are connected to someone who causes pain—for others and for himself—remember this: no person feels worse about something gone wrong than someone who prefers living in the right.

I can't remember meeting any person who gets up every day hoping and praying that he will bring pain into the daily experience of those around him. I don't doubt there are people out there who think that way, but the average person doesn't want the drama of having to recover from doing wrong to another.

When you encounter someone whose sin has caused another pain, just realize that there's not a lot you can say or do to make that person feel worse than he already feels about what he has done. There is something you can do, however, to bring healing and restoration: show him grace, the kind of grace God pours out on you when you really blow it.

LIFE ON THE EDGE

Be alert and of sober mind. Your enemy the devil prowls
around like a roaring lion looking for someone to devour.
1 PETER 5:8

Hundreds of years ago a king started a search for a professional carriage driver to take him on his journeys to conduct his personal and business affairs. On the posting, applicants were instructed to apply in person at the king's office in the central court building.

Three men applied.

When the first applicant arrived for his interview, the king told him about the dangers of the job and then asked him one question: "Sir, my estate is high atop a mountain ridge, and not only is the only road accessing my home narrow, but there is no shoulder. In some places, if you were to run a carriage wheel even a few inches off the roadway, we would face certain death from falling hundreds of feet to the canyons below. The problem is, bandits know that this road is narrow, and several times a year we will most certainly face would-be robbers. If we slow down, they will steal whatever fortunes I am carrying that day, and my family will be placed in danger. Therefore, we must travel at a high rate of speed and cannot slow down. So my question is, knowing that the road is curvy and there is no margin for error, how close to the edge are you willing to travel?"

The first applicant replied, "My king, I am a professional driver. I would be willing to travel within three feet of the edge at a high rate of speed."

The king posed the same scenario and question to the second applicant, and he replied, "My king, I am an incredibly competent driver, and I'd be willing to drive within eighteen inches of the edge at a high rate of speed." The king thanked both men and told them they would receive a response later in the day, when the interviews were over.

When the third applicant arrived, the king confronted him with the same scenario, to which he responded, "My king, didn't you say that your family would be traveling with you several days a week? I know they mean more to you than life itself, and even on the days when you don't have your family on board, you are irreplaceable to your family, to our country, and to everyone who loves you. Since I'll be carrying such precious cargo, I would think you would want me to stay as far away from the edge as humanly possible."

The king gently exhaled in relief and immediately gave the position to this wise man.

The problem with so many of us men is that we think we have it within us to live life close to the margins of sin without stepping over the line. When there is no margin for error, mistakes are massive. Stay away from the edge.

THE FASTEST WAY TO DEFUSE A BOMB

There are very few things we all have in common. One thing we all share, however, is the pain and consequences we suffer over mistakes—our own and those of others.

No man is immune to failure. We fail our wives and our sons and daughters. We fail one another and we fail our employers. We even fail God.

Having an employment history that includes occasional failures, I know this: my first reaction to failure is often to put myself into overdrive so I can minimize the damage. I'm amazed at how creative I can be in justifying my offense, or in redefining what really happened, or in simply trying to bury the issue altogether—so that we can all move on like it never happened.

While the context has nothing to do with personal failure, there's a phrase in Acts 11:18 that fits here very well: "repentance that leads to life."

Life, as in repentance that does not lead to death—no deeper remorse, no further deception, no further humiliation, no further complicating the situation.

Repentance leads to life, to joy and fulfillment. And fresh starts.

The older I get, the more I understand that the best way to minimize the damage done when I make a mistake is to refuse to make excuses and to admit it immediately and reconcile it quickly.

Think about how many times you've encountered situations when a mistake or a sin would not have caused nearly so much damage, and would have ended far more gently, had the offender simply owned the error and reconciled it quickly.

Repentance breeds life.

A CRAFTSMAN WITH A VISION

But we have this treasure in jars of clay to show that
this all-surpassing power is from God and not from us.
We are hard pressed on every side, but not crushed;
perplexed, but not in despair; persecuted, but not
abandoned; struck down, but not destroyed.

2 Corinthians 4:7–9

What I wouldn't give to meet the man who first had the vision of Kintsugi, the Japanese art in which the artist takes a broken or fractured piece of pottery and repairs it using gold-laced epoxy. What was once something broken now has both a story and a future. A piece built for everyday function increases in value and has a fresh purpose only because it has been broken and put back together.

In my mind, I see this man standing in his kitchen, looking down at a fractured bowl sitting at his feet. He and his wife had picked it up at an open market during their first year of marriage, and they had used it every night at dinner. Now it's just an everyday household item that is broken, worthless, and fit to be tossed in the trash bin. But then a thought flashes through his mind: *Wait. What if. . .*

Jesus does something very much like this for those of us who are wounded and hurting because of sin.

Knowing that truth, why should you be ashamed of your wounds, especially since everyone has them? Why try to hide something you know we all share? Your pain and your areas of darkest shame can become your strongest and most effective platform for rescuing vast numbers of people who desperately need the healing and fresh start Jesus offers. When you have experienced the pain of brokenness hitched to the joy of redemption, God will connect you with people still traveling the road of despair—if only you will allow Him to do it.

When you decide that your past cannot own your future, when you determine that the cracks in your story are now laced with the Refiner's gold, then the Master Craftsman can place you in the lives of others still walking that journey. You'll encounter their lives at the crossroads of epic failure and decision. They can continue walking in failure, or they can decide to head out of it.

The sign posted at the crossroads is a living billboard advertising fine art…and that billboard is you. By God's sovereign design, you will encounter people as a fellow traveler who knows what the road to redemption looks like, because you dared to travel it.

At that crossroads, you may be the only one they'll listen to, simply because you have earned the right to be heard. You have traveled their road, but you've also traveled the road they've not traveled at this point: the road to redemption.

DRAMA AND A QUESTION
WORTH ASKING

If it is possible, as far as it depends on you,
live at peace with everyone.
ROMANS 12:18

Working with micromanagers has never been easy for me. I'm not a guy who sweats the tiniest details, and people who do sweat the small stuff make me sweat too—usually with some internalized anger, mixed with a pinch of bitterness, and marinated in thoughts of retaliation.

Then again, I'm sure I make others sweat all the more. I'm sure they have had to talk with God about me—about attitude adjustments I need to make.

The scripture verse above tells us that we should do everything we can to live and work in peace with everyone around us. So when we're faced with a potential conflict, we need to ask ourselves, "Is this battle worth fighting?"

I'm amazed at how often I find, when I step back and try to be objective, that a particular battle isn't worth fighting, simply because it never should have been a battle in the first place. It was more like a small skirmish, a little rift that popped up on my life's radar then was gone as fast as it appeared. I've found that these little dramas were things that, in the bigger picture of the kingdom of God, really didn't matter.

I've learned through experience that I can live in peace with others more easily when I am at peace with God. Said another way, when I choose to trust God with the outcome, peace resides in my heart. When my heart is content, my attitude tends to follow.

LOAFING

My soul followeth hard after thee.
PSALM 63:8 KJV

Loafing is a fine art unto itself, but when it comes to following after a holy God, loafing wasn't meant to be grafted into our DNA.

David speaks of following hard after God. A life that follows hard after God is a life lived with intention, a life free of distractions. Sadly, in the end David was not able to live up to the standards of a distraction-free spiritual life.

Spiritual loafing—following after God in a casual way—is far more dangerous than it may seem. By its very nature, loafing is rolling through life by impulse and with no real plan or concerns. It's just letting things fall where they may.

Live life long enough in a casual relationship with God, and you'll wind up exploring diversions that can take you further than you wanted to go, cost you more than you wanted to pay, and keep you longer than you intended to stay.

THEY CAME BACK—WITH JOY

We live in a hand sanitizer culture in which everything is expected to be germ-free. I can understand why people want to avoid germs, but I sometimes wonder if this hasn't made us a little soft in other areas of life—specifically in our walk with Jesus.

Danger is a reality of life for the true disciple, but I sometimes wonder if we Jesus followers have somehow come to believe that the Master wasn't speaking literally when He said, "If they persecuted me, they will persecute you also" (John 15:20).

In Luke 10, we read of Jesus sending people out into battle. Think about the soberness of it: they were going out on a straight-up odyssey, where the only agenda for the day was to wake up, get in the fight, and see what happened. He warned them that He was sending them out "like lambs among wolves" (verse 3) and that they were not to take anything with them.

Something amazing happened when these men returned from their assignment: "The seventy-two returned with joy and said, 'Lord, even the demons submit to us in your name'" (verse 17). They came back with joy, not beaten down or discouraged. They experienced real fulfillment.

Why the joy? Because they were living with a God-ordained purpose and not living out a manufactured dream based on their own set of goals. They were obedient to God, and obedience is the birthplace of vision.

God gave them a vision, and they acted on it. Then and only then did they find the kind of fulfillment that springs from the joy of walking in the power of the Holy Spirit.

"THOSE" PEOPLE

*And he did not do many miracles
there because of their lack of faith.*
MATTHEW 13:58

"Never take what was normal in the book of Acts as normal for today."

I was sitting in a seminary classroom almost twenty years ago when a professor said those words to a group of young, green men filled with energy and wanting to get moving in their kingdom careers. He was a good man and I liked him.

I know exactly what he was trying to say. You see, there's this vibe in evangelicalism, especially within my tribe, the Baptists, that people who lean Pentecostal or charismatic are sort of slower to get it.

To put it a different way, here in the South, when we feel sorry for somebody who doesn't "get it," we just say, "Bless his heart." That's Southern code for referring to someone who's, to put it gently, just a little behind.

By the way, I know that those people—those tambourine-toting, glory-to-God, amen-hallelujah-happy people—think the same thing about us. And they "bless our hearts" all the time.

What my professor brother was trying to say was that just because God gave people the ability to lay hands on a person and heal him back in New Testament times, don't expect that to happen right now. Just because God gave people visions to relay to the body of Christ then, don't look too hard for visions now, because if you do, people will think you're weird. And just because God gave people the super-natural ability to prophesy back then, don't try doing that now on Sunday before the offering, because church folk will think you are bipolar and say things like, "Honey, are you okay?"

Two decades ago, I bought into that line of thinking, but I don't buy into it anymore, for I know this to be true: if you don't expect anything from God, don't be surprised when your expectations are met.

EXPECTING THE EXPECTED

When the disciples James and John saw this,
they asked, "Lord, do you want us to call fire
down from heaven to destroy them?"
Luke 9:54

One of the things I love most about the scriptures is that God didn't make any attempt to cover up our inescapable humanity. One passage—Luke 9:51–56—contains a great example of this truth. In this case, Jesus gets the cold shoulder from a Samaritan village, and when James and John get wind of it, they are ready to "cowboy up."

"Lord, do you want us to call fire down from heaven to destroy them?" they asked Him (Luke 9:54).

James and John wanted to stomp on these people—not with whips, not by stoning them, and not with an old-fashioned beat-down. No, they wanted to literally flip the light switch of God's wrath and engulf them with actual fire from Jehovah God.

I have to admit that this verse gives me incredible hope as a man. That's because there's not much difference between you and me and these two disciples. We are men, and we get really, really angry—and sometimes for the right reasons. James and John believed they were speaking out of love for Jesus, standing up for Him, and defending the man they knew to be the One whom God had sent to their perverse generation.

Luke records that Jesus turned to James and John and rebuked them for what they had just suggested. What I wouldn't give to know what He said to them!

I love the irony in this passage. James and John were

following a man from Nazareth who was teaching them to love people, and the moment things didn't go their way, the moment people started acting ugly, they doubled down on the ugly meter in their sheer desire to kill 'em all.

The reality is this: one of the hardest lessons we as Jesus followers must learn is that lost people are going to act like lost people. Jesus calls us to do exactly what He did and love 'em anyway.

THE MOST UNLOVING THING

Brothers and sisters, if someone is caught in a sin,
you who live by the Spirit should restore that person gently.
But watch yourselves, or you also may be tempted.
GALATIANS 6:1

I seriously hate negative energy. If there is even the remotest possibility that a conversation I need to engage in might turn sour, or if I'm in a situation in which I need to confront someone, it can keep me up at night.

For many years, I allowed my feelings about negative energy to keep me from confronting people—those in my personal life and those on my work team—over behaviors, attitudes, or lifestyles that kept them from thriving.

Here's the reality: love wasn't created to operate in a context of neglect. You cannot love well while neglecting to come alongside people and speak out when you see them engaging in destructive attitudes and behaviors.

I believe the most unloving thing a brother can do to another brother is to leave him to walk alone on a path that ultimately leads to destruction.

DWELL WELL

Finally, brothers and sisters, whatever is true, whatever is noble, whatever is right, whatever is pure, whatever is lovely, whatever is admirable—if anything is excellent or praiseworthy—think about such things.

PHILIPPIANS 4:8

The mind is a wild and fascinating creature unto itself. I am forever amazed at the truth that a man's mind holds within it the capacity for such greatness while at the same time being the breeding ground for so much depravity. I am fully convinced that how we live life, in relationship to God and to one another, is a battle fought in the mind.

Every man has won. . .and lost. . .many battles in the mind. Attitudes come and go, and lust is never more than a split second away as it waits for a chance to get in the game. Apathy, neglect, humility, and other responses to our circumstances all run through our minds. I wish I had a playbook for how a man could go undefeated in every season of life when it comes to the mind. I do know this, however: a man's mind lives in the ebb and flow of what he allows it to dwell on.

Today, when you encounter a victory of any sort, dwell on the power of God that brought that victory to you. And if you should experience failure, even of the smallest kind, dwell, too, on the power of Jesus, who paid the price so that you can have ultimate victory.

HE COMES IN THE CLOUDS

"Look, he is coming with the clouds."
REVELATION 1:7

Battles, struggles, difficulties, and complex situations are often referred to as "storms." The natural reaction for any follower of Jesus when he's faced with such a storm is to simply get through it in hopes of better days. There's even a cliché for it: weather the storm.

Weathering a storm is a decent game plan, and no one would argue that it shows anything but resolve. Weathering can, in fact, produce true grit.

True disciples, however, must learn to do more than just survive a storm. They must make sure they don't spurn the experience by simply putting their heads down and standing their ground. When the head is down, so are the eyes, and a man can't see the activity of heaven when his vision is cast upon his shoes.

The next time you see storm clouds on your horizon, do not spurn the coming rains. Instead, welcome them as yet another experience that can enrich your love for God and your trust in His mighty hand.

Storms are essential to the growth and health of any ecosystem. Constant sunshine only produces a barren desert land full of thorns and thirst. The same holds true for the health and growth of your relationship with Christ.

John was exiled to an island called Patmos for what his accusers felt sure was deserved torture; yet while he was there, he recorded the words in the book of Revelation. It may be that John could not hear God speak until he got away from the muck and routine of everyday life. It may be that God knew that John needed worship in order to hear Him, so He placed him upon an island where, in his own words, "I was in the Spirit" (Revelation 1:10).

Storms are not what they appear when you follow in the footsteps of a sovereign God.

A STRUGGLE COMMON TO ALL MEN

*Blessed are those who fear the L*ORD*, who find great delight
in his commands. Their children will be mighty in the land;
the generation of the upright will be blessed. Wealth and
riches are in their houses, and their righteousness endures
forever. Even in darkness light dawns for the upright,
for those who are gracious and compassionate and righteous.
Good will come to those who are generous and lend freely,
who conduct their affairs with justice.*

PSALM 112:1–5

Most men I know struggle with selfishness. I would include myself in that appraisal. In fact, I sometimes wonder if I could win an induction into the Hall of Fame for selfishness.

There are those men who truly do not care about anyone but themselves, regardless of the situation. However, I believe that sort of man is a rare breed.

If you were to treat selfishness like an apple and peel it down to its core, I believe you'd find that most selfishness is born of fear. I believe selfishness is actually fear—specifically, the fear that we won't get what we think is best for us—in disguise. That fear motivates us to manipulate situations and people. Regardless of how our actions affect other people, we often act selfishly because we are more concerned about *out-come* than about the *people* nearest to us.

This is insecurity at its worst. Believe me, I know this beast well, as I've lived with it for years.

The selfishness born of fear always comes back home to doubts over the sovereignty of God. If I believe God will always take care of me, then I will be free to put others first because I know He will always give me what I need.

Take your time and reread the passage above. Read it through the lens of someone who has given himself over to the freedom God's sovereignty brings.

THE LAND OF SOUR

Have the same mindset as Christ Jesus.
PHILIPPIANS 2:5

My attitude dictates how I respond to virtually everything I encounter. The problem is that my attitude can sometimes go sour so fast that it takes a hefty charge of power from God's Spirit to generate the current necessary to bring me back into my native land, where His peace and joy reside.

I hate living, even for a solitary hour, in the Land of Sour. I hate allowing my mind to go there and dwell. I hate when I allow someone or something to own my emotions. I should never allow any person, object, or situation to own my emotions. I know that only God holds the deed to that property, yet I fail on this front more times than I care to admit. When my attitude goes sour, it is most often my witness for Christ that takes the blow. It is a painful thing to realize that I've allowed my attitude to set me back in the way I relate to those who are without Christ.

Sometimes a man's attitude fails him because he's trying to control a situation instead of trusting in God to work things out in His time. Then there are times when a man's attitude goes sour simply because he lets someone or something penetrate his heart and bend his will in the direction of disdain.

The Land of Sour, regardless of how one may arrive there, is no place to live for a man who is a resident of heaven living for now on this side of the river. The good news is that we don't have to wait for the day when we cross that final stream in order to experience the joy of Jesus in the here and now.

A MATTER OF *OUGHT*

I asked him to tell me about his family, but he couldn't. He had been told that he had brothers and sisters, but he had no idea of their whereabouts. He didn't know where his mother was living and he'd never met his father. Born in Europe's poorest country, Moldova, he was yet another forgotten child being raised in a shelter that had become his home. He had nowhere else to go.

He was at the end of the line. . .at the mere age of eight years old.

I'm often asked, "Why do you go to Moldova?" In almost every investigation of my heart, the answer to that question eludes me. I suppose the underlying question for every one of us is, "Why do you do *anything* you do?"

There are many things I could do, yet there's a difference between what I *could* do and what I *should* do. At the heart of the reason for my expeditions to Moldova is a simple answer: God told me to go. Upon that command, I had to go because it was no longer a matter of desire, but of obedience, and my desire is to be obedient.

There I am, standing in a shelter in a former Soviet country, looking into the eyes of this young boy. It's a strange animal, this thing we call abandonment. I cannot speak about it personally, for I've never felt its attack.

I have on many occasions stood only feet away and watched as this animal fed on the souls of those who are defenseless. I cannot look away from it, cannot pretend not to see it. I cannot pretend as if I am helpless to do anything about it.

There are times in life when I could do something but I don't. We've all been there. When it comes to being a messenger of justice and mercy, however, it is not only something I *could* do but something I *should* do.

You will probably never go to work with orphans in Moldova, but that has no bearing on whether you are able to be a messenger of justice and mercy. You are called to uphold justice and mercy everywhere you go. You ought to do it, and you should do it, because the God who created you has told you to do it.

It's a matter of *ought*.

A TARGET DEFINED

Most days during the school year I drive my older son, Cole, to school. I cherish this short commute because it gives me a chance to talk with him and to see life through the eyes of a young boy. Our conversations range from hunting, to homework, to the latest item on the school lunch menu, to why classic rock is critical to humanity, and, occasionally, to girls. I've discovered that girls in the new millennium do, in fact, still have "cooties." Not much has changed on that front.

As we drive up to the school, I usually ask Cole the same question: "Which is better, to be the head or the tail?" He knows the question is coming, so he gives me a ready answer: "The head, because the view is better." When he grabs his book bag and exits the truck, I say to him, "Be a leader today, bud." It's a simple exercise I will not give up on because I want Cole to be conscious of leadership, even though he's a young boy.

To build upon this, Cole and I started a fun exercise this past summer. In trying to coax him into the conversation, I said, "Hey, Cole, let's spend some time together this summer trying to define manhood and the qualities it takes to be a real man of God."

He responded, "Dad, why would you want to define what it means to be a man when you're already a man?" It's a great point, so I explained to him that when you don't know what your target is, it's impossible to hit it. He seemed to understand why a man must define his pursuits, so I asked him, "What do you think it means to be a man, Cole?" His answer stunned me, because I didn't expect an eight-year-old to plow so deep.

He said, "I think a man should be loyal." I asked him

why he chose loyalty, and he said, "Well, let's say one of your friends is hurting, or something has happened. I think a real man doesn't leave someone stranded." I really didn't know what to say.

A moving target is hard to hit, but an undefined target is impossible to hit. For years, I had general ideas of what biblical manhood looked like, but I had never truly defined my target.

It's been said that "a goal without a plan is just a wish." I don't want to *wish* I was a man of God. I want to *know* I am a man of God, and live like a man of God, because I have a concrete understanding of biblical manhood. Such an understanding will come only if I carve out my manhood from the pages of scripture.

I am looking forward to my father-son journey with Cole to define manhood. Judging from the way things have started, I am not always going to be the one doing the teaching.

WITHERED

"Remain in me, as I also remain in you. No branch can bear fruit by itself; it must remain in the vine. Neither can you bear fruit unless you remain in me. I am the vine; you are the branches. If you remain in me and I in you, you will bear much fruit; apart from me you can do nothing. If you do not remain in me, you are like a branch that is thrown away and withers; such branches are picked up, thrown into the fire and burned."

JOHN 15:4–6

Every sport has its legends. When I was a young boy, my dad talked about the larger-than-life personas of men like Mickey Mantle and Roger Maris. Growing up in the game of golf, I had a chance to view men like Jack Nicklaus, Arnold Palmer, and Greg Norman in that same regard. They were humans, yes, but they were not like the rest of us. Watch Jack Nicklaus hit a golf ball, and you realize that we are not, in fact, all created equal.

The world of hunting has its legends too. Men like Teddy Roosevelt and Fred Bear helped shape the sport. There are other legends as well, who unlike the late Fred Bear, still walk among us. Two of these giants are Harold Knight and David Hale, pioneers of the hunting community who helped shape an industry that thrives today.

I was recently honored to share a turkey hunt with Knight and Hale. As we watched the Kentucky sun rise over ridges that held thundering toms at roost, David and Harold noticed that a group of toms were using a small field perched high on top of a ridge, so we built a makeshift blind to provide some cover as we waited for the hunt to unfold. We cut branches from oak and maple trees that were beginning to grow foliage.

As I sat in this blind behind the camera, I couldn't help but notice how the leaves of these freshly cut branches began to wither in only a matter of about two hours. Strong, broad, beautiful leaves were now curling and withering before my very eyes. What were once bright, green, thriving leaves were now dulling in color because of one simple truth: they were cut off from the source that gave life to their cells.

It is true that we are not all equals when it comes to talent, and that is why some men reach legendary status in golf, baseball, and, yes, even hunting. The reality, however, is that while talent may separate us when it comes to sports, we are all united in the truth that every man will wither apart from the life-giving Spirit of Jesus Christ. The absence of His life flowing through a man's veins will easily tell on him, for he will be withered and dull if he allows himself to detach from the very God who created him.

THE POWER OF A PLAN

For we wanted to come to you—certainly I, Paul, did,
again and again—but Satan blocked our way.
1 THESSALONIANS 2:18

You see both sides of manic when you're in the presence of Jesus followers and someone mentions the idea of making a plan. There are those who believe that God uses a prepared mind, and thus failing to plan is planning to fail. Then there are those who believe that planning is a surefire way to have the Holy Spirit walk right out of your life. There is some truth to both sides of the argument.

My conviction is this: you can plan the Spirit right out of your life just as easily as you can blame the Holy Spirit for the results of all your impulsive, knee-jerk reactions that have caused you to chase every new thing as something "God wants me to do."

If you know anything about the life of the apostle Paul, you know that he set sail many times, from many ports, to carry the Gospel of Jesus to those who'd not yet heard it. However, there were times when his plans morphed because things changed.

You cannot convince me that Paul woke up one day and decided on impulse to sail to Ephesus. I've never lived in a world where boats were basically the only form of transcontinental travel, but I can assure you that no man in his right mind just goes on a hiatus to share the Gospel without making some kind of plan—especially in a world where you can't just catch a flight back home if things go bad.

Every great leader I've ever known has had, on some level, some form of a plan to accomplish what God had called him to do. I cannot remember meeting anyone who has heard a call from God that did not come with some sort of qualifier. Yes, Abraham was told to walk, and that's all he was told. However, instances like that are few and far between. More often than not, when God gives you a calling, it comes with some sort of direction or instruction.

So pray hard, pray long, be patient, and move slowly. Then, once you get that word from God, act on it. Start moving—and if God wants to change your direction, He'll let you know. The world won't change when Jesus followers are frozen in fear over "missing the will of God" and thus decide to stay on the porch instead of moving out.

SHOUTING AT THE DARKNESS

Over the past year or so, I've faced many battles being fought mostly in the mind. Honestly, I have to say that I lost many of those battles as I became overly focused on what I view as deeply troublesome issues facing our country today. Sometimes all I could think about was how ruined our country seems—spiritually, morally, and financially. I would find myself feeling angry, feeling helpless when it came to doing anything to help our country regain its compass.

The problem has been that I've allowed myself to engage in behavior I have preached against for many years. I have warned Christians that they should never find themselves guilty of what I call "shouting at the darkness." Yet it seemed that warning never applied to me.

We Christians have a way of shouting at darkness for being dark. We shout at darkness when we see moral decay and unrighteous living around us. Those things are certainly dark, and they make for easy targets. But here's the truth: no matter how much we shout at the darkness for being so dark, the darkness remains the same—dark.

I've realized that when I spend my energy shouting at the darkness, the only thing that changes is my attitude—for the worse. When I do that, my attitude doesn't reflect the joy of Jesus, and my words are full of nothing but anger and disgust.

I've figured out that I must share the light of Christ, not curse the darkness for being dark. I must tell anyone who will listen that there is a better way, and His name is Jesus. My prayer lately has not been that I'll just "be positive" for the sake of being positive. My prayer is that the joy of Jesus will so fill my thoughts and my attitude that I won't be distracted by the darkness, but rather filled with His light.

I am winning more, and losing less, in these battles in my mind. It hasn't been easy, but I will keep trying, because I've figured out that shouting about the Light is far better than shouting at the darkness.

HANDLING CRITICISM

*"What does this have to do with you, you sons of Zeruiah?
If he is cursing because the LORD said to him, 'Curse David,'
who can ask, 'Why do you do this?' "*
2 SAMUEL 16:10

Nobody likes being criticized—myself included. I cringe when someone offers me what they call "constructive criticism," because I know those words are usually followed by a rebuke, and sometimes an intensely personal one.

In 2 Samuel 16 we read of a man named Shimei, who did something beyond brave. Had Shimei merely protested, it would have been brave. But he came out of nowhere as King David passed a road near his home and began to throw rocks and curse David's leadership as king. In fact, one of David's servants offered to cut off Shimei's head to shut him up.

Most every other king in David's position would have given his servant the green light, but David did not. He listened to the man and pondered his words. In the end, David asked himself, "Could he be right?"

Having been in ministry and leadership for over twenty years, I've had my fair share of critics. My wife has forever been an asset to me, and that includes taking the time to talk to me after such ego demolitions. When I tell her about the criticism I've received, she'll gently say, "Well, let's try to work through it and see if there is actually any truth to it."

I don't like my wife much in those moments—not much at all.

The truth is that every great leader knows that greatness doesn't come through blanket praise. Greatness is forged in struggle, and sometimes those struggles involve asking yourself, "Could my critics be right?"

PRAYING A DIFFERENT WAY

"You may ask me for anything
in my name, and I will do it."
JOHN 14:14

A transition has happened in how I pray about what's ahead of me. I had always prayed for wisdom and then set my goals for doing what I thought needed to be done in my life and ministry.

Then one day, a wise friend (one I literally consider a modern-day prophet) challenged me to think about this: "What if God doesn't want you doing *any* of the things you think need to be done?" I wondered if maybe I had been asking for God's direction, but in reality I was basically saying to Him, "Hey, this is what I'm going to do, so please bless it." My intentions may have been good, but not necessarily in line with God's heart.

I recently began to pray this way: *God, reveal to me what You want for my life this year, and I'll set those revelations as my primary goals.*

That's a different way to pray altogether. Jesus told us that if we ask God for anything in His name, He will do it for us. But how do we know if we are praying in line with the heart of God? We've all prayed for things that never came to pass, so were we wrong in how we were praying? Maybe. . .maybe not.

So who knows the heart of God best? Answer: He does. He knows what He wants to do in my life, so the only way I can know if I am praying in line with His will is to ask Him to reveal His heart to me. When He does that for me, then I can begin praying accordingly.

I asked God to reveal to me His heart for my life, and He began to cause two specific things to float to the top in my spirit: my family and my health. God showed me that He wanted me to make those two areas my top priorities, so I locked my focus on them. I was amazed as I started to see His hand moving in some beautiful ways. I became more in tune with Michelle's heart, and after getting a physical, I finally realized why I'd been battling fatigue for so long.

The only way you can know for sure that you're praying in accordance with the heart of God is to stop pursuing any and every course and then just wait for Him to reveal what He wants for you. Be willing to toss aside the need to know *why* He's revealing a specific course of action and start walking in the revelation He's given you. Let Him guide your priorities, and you'll experience in a big way what it means to "walk in the Spirit."

BROTHERS

Growing up, I often heard people refer to various church-going men as "Brother Jim" or "Brother Wayne." As the years progressed and I began to pastor, people often wanted to call me "Brother Jason." It drove me nuts—and it still does. I asked people to call me "Jason" because "Brother Jason" seemed artificial and weird to me.

To be candid, it wasn't the average churchgoer calling me "Brother Jason" that bothered me so much, because I realized that was their way of showing respect for my calling. The irk came from preachers who couldn't seem to pronounce it without saying it like this: "Bratherrrrr Jason"—with what sounded to me like a silky smooth and self-righteous tone. It just didn't fit me or my generational vibe.

When the apostle James wrote his letter, which eventually became part of scripture, he used the word *brothers* or *brethren* no fewer than thirteen times. The word comes up over and over again and is a calling out of sorts, a reminder that we are in this thing together.

In the original language, this word is literally "brothers of mine." We often say "my brother," but James calls me "brother of mine"—flesh of my flesh and part of a "tribe" (see James 1:1). It's a clear understanding that we are joined—banded together in this journey by the understanding that a man named Jesus unites us as we move through life together.

I cannot imagine James calling me "Bratherrrrr Jason." I think if we ran into each other at the store, he'd just say, "Hey, brother."

ASKING FOR WISDOM

But when you ask, you must believe and not doubt, because the one who doubts is like a wave of the sea, blown and tossed by the wind. That person should not expect to receive anything from the Lord. Such a person is double-minded and unstable in all they do.
JAMES 1:6–8

James 1:5 tells us that any man who wants wisdom from the heart of God must simply ask Him for it, and God will certainly give it to him. But James qualifies the promise, telling us that the man who wants wisdom must ask in faith without doubting and that if he doubts, he can't expect to receive anything from God.

When a man asks for wisdom, it's usually in connection to a specific situation. But did you notice that James tells us that doubting men are "unstable" not just in one situation, but in "all they do"?

A doubting, unstable man cannot be trusted. That's why it's not wise to hitch your wagon to someone who over-reacts emotionally, often changes his mind, and never follows through on anything.

An unstable man is not just unstable; he's unwise. His doubting nature causes him to be constantly "tossed around" with indecision. Therefore, he can ask for wisdom, but he won't get it.

Receiving wisdom is a twofold process: you ask for wisdom, and then you ask God to give you courage to follow through on what He reveals to you. When you ask for wisdom, ask God to reveal the next step, and when He does, take that step in faith—even if it doesn't seem logical. Show the Lord—and yourself—that you are not a doubting man. Then you can be sure that God will light your path.

GUILT. . .OR GUILT RIDDEN?

*Godly sorrow brings repentance that leads to salvation
and leaves no regret, but worldly sorrow brings death.*
2 Corinthians 7:10

For those genuinely grafted into the vine of Christ, sin brings about guilt. If it doesn't, then a man has a much larger problem than the sin he's committed. Sin brings guilt, or "godly sorrow," which leads to repentance. This kind of guilt is your best friend and a guide in the vast wilderness of humanity, for it drives you to find shelter in the eternal heart of God, which is fortified in forgiveness.

If only we could put guilt in its proper place. More often than not, we let guilt take up residence in our lives and allow it to stay in our dwelling places right alongside us every day. When that happens, it's not a righteous guilt sprung forth from a heart inhabited by Christ. Instead, "godly sorrow" becomes bondage that keeps you from the heart of God and the grace that's found there.

When you sin, don't fight the guilt. Let it drive you to the heart of the Father. If, however, you find yourself still walking in shame later on, change your prayer life from one seeking forgiveness to one seeking freedom.

THE PURPOSE OF GOD'S PROVISION

Then the LORD said to Moses,
"I will rain down bread from heaven for you."
EXODUS 16:4

Any man worth his spiritual salt would be quick to testify to the truth that our God provides, but we need to understand that God doesn't continuously provide just to make life easier on us.

As God's people trekked through the wilderness after their exodus from Egypt, they became hungry. Hunting is hard enough, but I cannot imagine trying to feed a family on what you can drag home from the desert floor. God provided for His people something called "manna"—bread from heaven.

While God wanted to keep His people from starvation, His greater purpose in providing manna for His people was to teach them of His sovereign ability to provide not just food, but everything else they needed to make it through life.

God doesn't waste an experience. He takes you through all of life's experiences, giving you your own version of a cloud to follow by day and fire by night to navigate the unknown. He's showing you His strength for your future Jordan River moments of crisis, moments when you need to remember that He is able.

ALL NIGHT LONG

Late one summer night, when I was around eight years old, my dad and I stayed up late to finish watching a movie on television. Then, out of nowhere, Dad looked at me and said, "Want to go fishing? Stay out till the sun comes up?" Fishing at night was no new thing to me, even at that age, for my dad loved fishing for smallmouth bass. He was good at it, too. A smallmouth is a finicky, bad-attitude bass, and when you throw scorching summer sun into the equation, your best option is to pursue them at night. It took all of about two-tenths of a second for me to go all in and accept the offer.

We fished all sorts of places that night, and we ended up in a little cove right by a roadside pullout. I can't remember if we were fishing from the boat that night, and I can't remember if we caught any fish. What I can recall, with a fresh-as-yesterday memory, is that we ended up wading knee deep in the water, without a rod in hand, and just played around, trying to stay awake until we watched the sun finally appear over the tree line.

Sometimes I think I'm guilty as a dad of overthinking what it means to create a memory. It's time spent, not how you spend it, that matters most.

MEN AND INFLUENCE

Most of my childhood memories are attached not just to golf itself, but to a specific course. The nine-hole course, filled with white oaks and pines, where my dad first entered the PGA program was, and forever is, like hallowed ground to me.

Every Saturday morning at the course, I'd stand at a distance and listen to a group of men discuss their morning round. They'd settle up their bets and spend the next few hours telling tales of how the game had once again handed them an unfair dose of reality.

These guys were giants in my eyes. They had their own stories, and man, how I loved listening to how they fought the war or how they landed a business deal during their prime! I'm sure none of them knew it, but each of them was forming a part of my story. To them, I'm sure it was nothing more than taking the time to talk to a kid who hung around the edges of their morning huddles. Having a special group of people let me know I was one of their own felt like my own version of the green Masters jacket.

Never underestimate the power you can have on a young life. You have no idea just how closely a young person is watching. . .and listening.

THE COUNSEL OF THE ALMIGHTY

Blessed is the one who does
not walk in step with the wicked.
PSALM 1:1

Self-awareness is a critical survival skill for any man. A man must be wise enough to realize that, like it or not, the attitudes and values of the men with whom he surrounds himself can influence him.

For me, Psalm 1 has been something of a spiritual GPS, always navigating me back on track. It reminds me of my vulnerability to the thoughts and opinions that others inject into my head.

Here's the bottom line: your best and closest confidants must be men filled with the power of God. You have the right to choose your crew, and you'd better choose valiant men who are wise with the counsel of the Almighty.

MONKEY STOMPING A BULLY

The LORD is the stronghold of my life—
of whom shall I be afraid?
PSALM 27:1

If you are high on the gift of mercy—and low on the gift of justice—you may want to skip this Man Minute. Just move on, because you're not going to like it.

My older son was about to start school, and I knew that sooner or later he'd have to deal with a bully. I just had no idea it would be in kindergarten. Cole came home one day and told me that a classmate had told him that he wanted one of Cole's baseball cards. Threatened with being, in the bully's words, "beat up," Cole gave him the card.

We'd had several talks about this before it ever happened, and I was beside myself as to why Cole didn't follow my counsel and knock this kid into next week. They were five years old, so how bad could a punch be? Cole eventually stood up to the kid, and as soon as that happened, the challenger backed down without even a hint of a struggle.

Weeks after the baseball card incident, we were at a parent-student activity, and I saw Cole's nemesis, whose dad happened to be there as well. The Man Minute is about straight-up, raw honesty. So here it is: my first thought when I saw this man was, *Friend, I'm about to monkey stomp you if you don't get your kid in line.*

Monkey stomp—you know, pound him like a gorilla using all fours to beat someone into submission. It's a beautiful picture, if you ask me, of the perfect marriage between brute strength and agility.

Do you ever wonder where it is those feelings of wanting to protect your kids come from? I can promise you, my thoughts of wanting to vindicate my son and protect him didn't come from the devil. God is a Father, a perfect one, and He protects His children. A father's heart for his kids isn't born in a vacuum, and he wants to protect them. It's a natural instinct to do whatever it takes to ensure the safety of your children.

Never forget that you are God's child and He will fight your battles for you. There's no monkey stomping I could ever give a guy that could equate to what the Lord of Hosts can do.

ALL A MAN'S WAYS

Proverbs 16:2 is a verse that continually provides me with real-time course correction. It states: "All a person's ways seem pure to them, but motives are weighed by the LORD." While my mind forever gravitates to the motive aspect of this verse, motive is just a mirror reflection of the first part of this scripture.

"All a person's ways. . ." That brings to center stage our ability to justify just about anything. Think about it. Time and time again, when we are faced with a decision, it is overtly simple to justify a choice that elevates our preferred position in the outcome. It's human nature to want to be the winner every time.

In the end, however, what guides your process must be an all-out rejection of self-justification. If you want to honor God with your decisions, you must surrender your will and pray yourself into a place where your heart wants nothing in it that isn't born in the heart of God.

GETTING WHAT YOU WANT

You have been set free from sin and
have become slaves to righteousness.
ROMANS 6:18

God has a history of giving us exactly what we want. You can find story after story in scripture testifying to the fact that God lets people have their own way. It started in the Garden of Eden. Adam and Eve wanted freedom, so God gave it to them. Even though the people of Israel had Samuel, they wanted "their own king," so God gave them Saul. The prodigal son wanted to go to town and do his own thing, and his dad let him do just that.

Often when I come to a crossroads in my journey of faith, a quiet and sober truth soaks into my heart: while I may say I want to obey the Lord, the truth is that I can do what I want. I can choose to do it my way, and nobody is going to stop me.

The problem with actually following through on what I want to do is that I cannot see the view from thirty thousand feet, like God can. I have limited perspective mixed with limited understanding—a bad combination for success. Perhaps that is what Paul was getting at when he said that he was a slave to righteousness—a freed man who is bound to serve the heart of God. Only when you and I find freedom in such bondage will we be able to overcome ourselves.

IT'S IN THE EYES

*And hope does not put us to shame, because God's
love has been poured out into our hearts through
the Holy Spirit, who has been given to us.*
ROMANS 5:5

Not long ago, I boarded an airbus to Eastern Europe for a mission trip to work with kids, and their adult leaders, who live in orphanages. For almost a decade, the church we attend has been dedicated to working to bring hope to these kids.

One of my first impressions of this former Soviet Union region was that the main city where we stayed, Chișinău (pronounced Keesh-now), was a city struggling for survival. The city bustled with life, and while parts of it were modern, some of it seemed tired from the struggle.

After I'd interacted with some of the folks who lived there—from the airport employees to the servers at the restaurants—it occurred to me that you could gaze into the eyes of many of them and find a hollow, often expressionless look, the look of someone who is grinding it out every day.

Then I met the members of our host team, many of whom had grown up in the orphanages. They were from the same country, but the difference in their countenance was striking. Every one of them knew someone who had been trafficked into the sex slave trade. However, these people— many of them teenagers—were crazy animated, as if their lives were one big party after another. They were well kept and on their game—all smiles, hugs, and jokes.

When I looked into their eyes, I could see the difference Jesus makes in the souls of people whose thirst for hope has been quenched.

A STRANGE UNION

From him the whole body, joined and held together
by every supporting ligament, grows and builds
itself up in love, as each part does its work.

EPHESIANS 4:16

Every time I'm around a group of believers who've come together for a cause—for example, a mission trip, a men's retreat, or an outdoor conference—I'm gripped by how radically different our stories are. Where each person comes from, how they got to this place in life, and how they ended up on this particular trip would appear to the typical observer to be wildly random. You and I both know, however, that "random" does not even fit into the equation.

I see the glory of God in its most evident light when groups like this come together. You see men, usually in the war of marketplace competition, swinging hammers side by side to fix someone's home. You see the upwardly mobile salesman sitting right next to a retired soldier in a hunting camp, both looking into the scriptures to find deeper truths that solidify the identity of their manhood.

The strange union around the campfire of brotherhood is not so strange at all when you stop to consider the Guide who led each man to his place in the circle.

NEGLECT

Discipline your children, for in that there is hope;
do not be a willing party to their death.
PROVERBS 19:18

I found myself getting angry at the kid. He seemed to know the exact location of every one of my buttons labeled PUSH FOR INSTANTANEOUS NEGATIVE RESPONSE.

Later that night I realized I could not lay 100 percent of the blame for the boy's behavior on him. Sure, when he gets older, the blame will be all his, but for now, he's only about 30 percent to blame for his obnoxious behavior. The blame really goes to his mom and dad. They chalk it up to his constant "attitude," but I chalk it up to parents who are guilty of a form of neglect. That's right. Child neglect is what was really going on. His parents had neglected to show real love—for real love loves too much to withhold discipline.

Real love has boundaries. Real love cares enough to actually parent instead of just being a provider of things like toys, video games, and food. To be honest, I grieve a bit when I think of this boy's future. I grieve over the way he's going to treat his wife, over the way he's going to be talked about in the office. Most of all, I grieve for his mom and dad, for in a few short years they will reap what they've sown.

"DAD, I'M TALKING TO YOU"

I have many tendencies that are not so stellar. One of them is overcommitting myself simply because I want to experience all of life, and yet do it before lunch. I'm working on it, but it's not an easy thing for me.

One day my son Cole was sitting in the backseat of our vehicle as we drove into our neighborhood. I don't know what he was talking about, for I was thinking about some project I had to complete in the near future. However, I clearly heard, "Dad, I'm talking to you." Which he followed up with, "You know, Dad, sometimes lately, I've been talking but you're not listening."

The words were like an arrow shot straight to my soul. I told Cole I was sorry for not listening to him and that, yes, I'd been in my own little world lately. I promised to improve.

The thing about this crazy pace at which we all now live is that it doesn't just rob us of time. . .it robs those we love of our greatest contribution to their lives: our presence.

When I live from appointment to appointment, meeting to meeting, I am never fully present. I pretty much live in constant transit from one thing to the next, and those who feel it most are in the backseat.

ENDURANCE THAT PRODUCES

I suppose it can rightly be said of me, "He's not the sharpest tool in the shed, but he's still around." Maybe that could be a new start-up campaign for a nonprofit organization that helps kids who struggle academically but have lots of drive.

I've always said that I'm living proof that you can go all the way in education if you know how to get your hands on extra credit. Perseverance is one thing I know I have, and to be candid, I'd rather have perseverance than talent. I'd take heart over talent any day. After all, how many underachievers have you met who have crazy talent yet refuse to use it? My point exactly.

The apostle James tells us that when life brings tests our way, we should not scorn the classroom exercise because "the testing of your faith produces perseverance" (James 1:3).

James goes on to write, "Let perseverance finish its work so that you may be mature and complete, not lacking anything" (1:4). Walk backward through that verse for a second. If you want to be mature and complete, with an understanding that you are content and lacking nothing, you're going to have to obtain maturity. And the only way you obtain maturity is by learning how to persevere through the years and the experiences those years bring.

FRATE DE SUFLET

While I was in another country on a mission trip, I met Boris, our driver for the week. Driving was pretty much his full-time job. He had scraped up enough money to buy a nice eighteen-passenger van, and he used it to shuttle corporate customers during their stays in his country.

Boris was a funny guy, and he loved to pick on people. He was also incredibly patient with me. I am the man who likes to ask lots of questions. I love new experiences, and I love to learn about people and their own personal stories. So put me in a new country with new people, all of whom have their own personal stories, and I'm in full-throttle question mode. Boris fielded every question with grace and detail, helping me—the greenhorn American—to understand his culture.

I'm forever amazed at the bond of brotherhood that comes only through being in the family of God. Boris is more than a friend—he's my brother, for we are both followers of the man Jesus. Those bonds of brotherhood run deep, for they are sealed in an eternal blood covenant.

I told Boris he was my soul brother, and he told me that same phrase in his language is *frate de suflet*—brother of my soul. That's what amazes me the most: that even though there were language and cultural barriers, and we had grown up on different continents, Boris and I were instantly *fraţii de suflet*—and all because of a Galilean.

SHIBBOLETH

When Jephthah, one of Israel's judges, was in the heat of battle, he knew that impostors would try to cross the Jordan to escape his army (see Judges 12). That's why they invented the code word *Shibboleth*.

Enemies from Ephraim might be able to wear the right clothes and swear they were from Gilead, but there was one thing Jephthah knew no Ephraimite could fake: his accent. Give him a few years, and he might be able to master a new language, but in the heat of the moment, when these enemies were mixing themselves in with people from Gilead, these men pronounced "Shibboleth" like this: "Sibboleth." That's because people from Ephraim didn't know how folks from Gilead pronounced "Shibboleth."

A man can fake a lot of things. He can learn how to operate in a church culture, and he can learn how to quote scripture. A man can even fake a lifestyle, but when a man gets squeezed, what's been in him all along will inevitably come out.

If you were squeezed, would you have "Shibboleth"? Only you know.

NOT IF YOU'RE MY KID

"Which of you fathers, if your son asks for a fish,
will give him a snake instead?"
Luke 11:11

During His earthly ministry, Jesus seemed to be in a constant state of trying to drive home certain points with His disciples. Sometimes they got it; sometimes they didn't.

I like reading about the disciples and how they handled different situations, because it makes me feel better about myself. Think about it. When you read about how Peter wanted to fight instead of using reason, doesn't it make you feel a little better about yourself?

When teaching them about the heart of His Father, Jesus asked them a rather humorous question: "Which of you fathers would give your son a snake when he's asked for a fish?" It's not just a comical question, but also a question only a dad would get, for every dad knows there is a love for his kids that goes beyond words. Would I give my son a copperhead when he wanted food? Not if he's my kid. He's getting food.

God takes care of His kids, because that's what a father does. That's what Jesus was communicating. I think they got it this time.

YOU HAVE TO TRUST

If you've been around Christianity even casually for any length of time, then you have no doubt heard the phrase "You just have to trust God." But have you ever thought about *why* God wants your trust? It's not because God wants you to have less stress in your life, though having less anxiety can be a derivative of a trusting faith.

Jesus gave a simple insight into why trusting the Father is crucial to the spiritual journey when He said, "So do not worry, saying, 'What shall we eat?' or 'What shall we drink?' or 'What shall we wear?' For the pagans run after all these things, and your heavenly Father knows that you need them" (Matthew 6:31–32).

Did you spot it? *"For the pagans run after all these things."*

God is sovereign. He set the planets in motion, and He put life in your bones. He is fully capable, and fully deserving, of managing your life both here and now and in the hereafter. When we reject the Father's love by rejecting His sovereign reign, we live as if God doesn't exist. In that moment, we really are no different from a nonbeliever.

God calls us to be different, and that starts with fully trusting Him in all things.

OLD FRIENDS, NEW CHAPTERS

*And I heard a loud voice from the throne saying, "Look! God's
dwelling place is now among the people, and he will dwell with
them. They will be his people, and God himself will be with
them and be their God. 'He will wipe every tear from their eyes.
There will be no more death' or mourning or crying or pain,
for the old order of things has passed away."*

REVELATION 21:3–4

A while back, my wife and I attended my twenty-year
high school reunion. I had looked forward to this day
for months, for I really did miss the crew I ran with all those
years ago.

Most of the faces I saw had changed, and most of our
stories were vastly different from the ones we were writing
twenty years ago. The chapters were filled with victories and
defeats, and you could see evidence of both in people's eyes.

The beauty of it all was that we were together, and this
time around it seemed as if we really did want to talk to one
another. Our fifteen-year reunion had, for some reason, failed
to materialize, and for many of us, this was the first time
we'd seen one another in more than a decade. For that reason
alone, it was sweet to hug people, look into their eyes, meet
their spouses, and just catch up.

For the few days after the reunion, I could not help but
think of my classmates. Their faces filled my mind's eye. And
it made me think about heaven.

I'm always bothered at most people's idea of heaven, for
many seem to think of it as a great family reunion, when the
true star will be Jesus and not some uncle or business partner
we've not seen in thirty years.

I still cannot help but anticipate being able to share time with one another once we're in heaven. What a delight it will be to sit and talk, with no recollections of pain or disappointment. I eagerly await the timeless feeling that will be ours in Christ when we all can share lives that never age.

CLEAR VISION

It's a fact that not all optics are created equal. Cheap scopes produce cheap results, and inexpensive binoculars will perform inexpensively just when you need everything to be its best.

I learned something about great optics a long time ago: the great ones gather far more light than the cheap ones. You can look through my Epochs at first light or at dusk, and you'll think you've just purchased thirty minutes of daylight. In that instant, you are able to see what you never could have seen on your own. To this day I still find myself amazed by this simple wonder.

Over the years, this short passage in the first chapter of Ephesians has taken deep root in my spirit:

> I keep asking that the God of our Lord Jesus Christ,
> the glorious Father, may give you the Spirit of wisdom
> and revelation, so that you may know him better. I pray
> that the eyes of your heart may be enlightened in order
> that you may know the hope to which he has called you,
> the riches of his glorious inheritance in his holy people,
> and his incomparably great power for us who believe.
> EPHESIANS 1:17–19

I find myself going over this passage again and again in my mind, for it tells me that God is willing to grant me the ability to see what I could never see on my own. The apostle Paul's words inform me that God has actually given me the ability to see with my heart things I cannot see on the surface.

Only the power of God can give you the optics you need to cut through the surface glare of life so that you may see what He wants you to see.

EXPERIENCE AND REVELATION

I keep asking that the God of our Lord Jesus Christ, the glorious Father, may give you the Spirit of wisdom and revelation, so that you may know him better. I pray that the eyes of your heart may be enlightened in order that you may know the hope to which he has called you, the riches of his glorious inheritance in his holy people, and his incomparably great power for us who believe.

EPHESIANS 1:17–19

When Christ touches you, He touches *all* of you. He becomes Lord of the whole and not just the part. You cannot wrestle with the God-man and leave only partially affected. Jacob walked forever with a Jabbok limp, and he should have, for it was a lifelong reminder of an encounter with the living God.

In the Hebrew mind, the "heart" was the centerpiece of a man, the whole inward self—both the mind and the emotions.

Christian leadership has always been skeptical of experiential faith, but Christianity was largely based on experience, for men and women experienced God in the flesh, and not just the idea of Him. The problem is that people take experience too far and abuse it by constantly saying things like "God told me. . ." Many times I have believed that God told me something very specific, but I had to check my motive to determine who was doing the speaking.

On the other hand, there are those who believe that God has revealed everything He will about Himself in scripture alone. But if that were the case—and it's not—then why would we need a Holy Spirit who serves as our "Advocate" (John 14:26) to guide us in our journey with God?

In the Christian faith, experience and revelation are not enemies. In fact, they are brothers who cannot be separated—no matter how hard theologians may try.

JESUS IS COMING

*For the trumpet will sound, the dead will be
raised imperishable, and we will be changed.*

1 CORINTHIANS 15:52

Eschatology is a big word someone had to teach to me, for I never heard much about it in the small Tennessee town where I grew up. Eschatology, which is the study of how the world will end, can be quite the obsession for some people.

Trying to figure out just exactly "how" Jesus is going to make His glorious return has never kept me awake at night. I've never been that obsessed with studying it, mainly because I know for certain that Jesus is going to come back someday—and that's all I really need to know. However, Christ did give us some insights into the events leading up to this event, and those are definitely worth knowing.

I've had the return of Christ on my mind for a few years now, mainly because I see so many of the signs Jesus spoke of surrounding His return unfolding before my very eyes.

For example, Jesus said, "You will hear of wars and rumors of wars" (Matthew 24:6), and "Nation will rise against nation, and kingdom against kingdom. There will be famines and earthquakes in various places" (Matthew 24:7). Today, you just about can't turn on the news without hearing about wars, uprisings, and other conflicts around the world.

Jesus also said, "Because of the increase of wickedness, the love of most will grow cold" (Matthew 24:12). Can you think of a time in human history when injustice and selfishness were as rampant as they are right now?

Jesus warned about false prophets and deceivers, saying,

"For false messiahs and false prophets will appear and perform great signs and wonders to deceive, if possible, even the elect" (Matthew 24:24). Can you think of a time when there have been more deceivers out there, so much so that you can't even begin to keep up with them?

I could go on and on, but I'll finish with this thought: I do not believe we are in the "last days." I believe we are in the "last of the last days."

More and more preachers around the world are preaching on the return of Christ. Signs of the end are everywhere. Christians are praying for it, and I'm one of them. Words cannot express my intense longing that at any given moment the sky would split and Christ would get the glory due His name.

I'm not going to sell my truck (I need it right up until the second Jesus comes), and I'm not going to quit my job (I love what I do). But I am—in my heart and in my spirit, and sometimes even with my eyes—looking east often, waiting for the sound of that promised trumpet.

SELFISH AMBITION

For where you have envy and selfish ambition,
there you find disorder and every evil practice.
JAMES 3:16

God did me a great favor when He brought the woman who would become my wife into my life twenty years ago. Little did I know, however, that she would be the one primarily responsible for deconstructing my precious ego.

Now, I feel the need to offer this disclaimer: to understand what I just said, you need to realize what I was up against in my early years. I was an only child and the only grandchild on one side of my family. Stop right there, and you have the perfect storm for a soon-to-be adult with little hope of living in social harmony. Add to that the fact that I was the son of a PGA professional who therefore became obsessed with the game of golf, and you have in the making a man with an only-child disposition who was obsessed with a game that is all about self and personal performance. It doesn't take a degree in psychology to surmise that in most situations, whatever "it" was, you can be sure it was going to be about me.

Marriage, and the one I'm married to, quickly helped me see how destructive selfish ambition can be to this thing we call life.

Selfishness is an emotional baseball bat swung wildly into your circle of relationships. Swing that bat, and things are going to get broken. Selfishness breaks things, and those "things" tend to be real people who are capable of being bruised. The end result is, as James tells us, disorder and every evil practice that comes with it.

Thank God for my wife!

FEW THINGS LAST FOREVER

*Jesus Christ is the same yesterday
and today and forever.*
HEBREWS 13:8

I would argue that perhaps one of the greatest guarantees a man has in life is that nothing stays the same. Jobs come and jobs go. Friends enter our lives, and over time many will fade away. Money is made, and then lost, and then (we hope) made again. People die, and sometimes those who leave are very close to us.

Change often has to do with loss, and that's not always a bad thing. Many changes are painful but bring great relief when the soul stretch has subsided. Even still, every time our story changes, the change brings with it a feeling of uncertainty.

Life is full of insanely bitter defeats and incredibly sweet victories. There's no way around it, so don't fear it. God is the master genius of forming for us a journey in which few things stay the same. You need to praise Him for that, for it creates an awesome sense of dependency for our independent selves.

The great comfort in it all is that although many things in our lives can and do change, the one constant is Jesus Christ. He'll be the same today, tomorrow, and forever.

THE POWER OF PARTNERSHIPS

Let no one deceive you with empty words, for because of such things God's wrath comes on those who are disobedient. Therefore do not be partners with them. For you were once darkness, but now you are light in the Lord. . . . Have nothing to do with the fruitless deeds of darkness, but rather expose them . . . . Be very careful, then, how you live—not as unwise but as wise.
EPHESIANS 5:6–8, 11, 15

How do you turn a battleship? It's easier than you might think: constant pressure on a small rudder. Over a relatively short period of time, the rudder's pressure wins, even though it must turn a massive vessel.

This is also true in matters of faith—and in every area of life. Even though the pressure might be subtle, you eventually adopt the mentality of the people around you. Why? Because the people who have the closest access to your heart and mind shape how you think.

It's the word *partners* as it is used in the above passage that always stops me cold. That's because holiness is forever tied to the power of our partnerships. What we choose to watch on TV or listen to in music is our entertainment partner. Who we choose to read is our life-philosophy partner, because we allow that writer to shape our thoughts. All of this matters, because we give those producers and authors— as well as our friends, colleagues, and golf partners—access to the precious asset of our minds.

An unrighteous partnership will always cloud your ability to discern truth from error, which is why Paul tells us to live "not as unwise but as wise." Wise men tenaciously guard their lives against wrong influences because they desire to be tenaciously holy.

WHY GOD WANTS YOUR MONEY

"For where your treasure is, there your heart will be also."
Matthew 6:21

Does He? . . . Does God really want my money? Does He really need my earning power?

In a word, yes. God actually does want your money, but not for the reason the average man, looking from the outside in, would assume. God is not cash deficient, but He does want your money.

If you've been in the church culture for any length of time, you've most likely encountered the truth from Malachi 3 where God informs His people that they are robbing Him by refusing to tithe or actually withholding from the entire tithe. They were keeping some of the money for themselves.

Why have I done it at times?

Why have you been guilty of the same?

In a word, fear.

For others, in yet another word, power.

Many times we are simply afraid of what might happen if we actually gave 10 percent of our gross income to God. Could we make it? When you're looking at the numbers— and the numbers don't lie—it's hard to make the numbers fit when they tell you there is too much month at the end of the money.

There are some men who just refuse to tithe. They want to chart their own course, and that includes how they spend their money.

This is what I know: I know that God has never failed me. I know that God has more money than I can possibly fathom and that He is not cash deficient.

So, if you think about it, the bottom line for God instructing me, coaching me, mentoring me, and, yes, commanding me to bring Him at least 10 percent of my gross income must not be about money at all.

God does want my money, because He wants my heart. He doesn't want me to fear anything, because He knows fear infects all areas of my life—not just my finances. He wants control of my life, because He knows that every man has the tendency to make a power grab and the need to run his own affairs. God knows that kind of arrogance will ruin a man on many levels.

So, yes, God does want my money—and yours.

The mind-bending reality of it all is that after decades of following Jesus, I am speechless at what God can do for me using only 10 percent of my money compared to what I can do when I demand the lot of it.

Tithing is a window into your soul.

CARING ENOUGH

I recently listened to a podcast by Bill Hybels, a man who has been at the epicenter of global Christian leadership for the past three or four decades and the founder of Willow Creek Community Church, which is located on the outskirts of Chicago and is one of the best-known churches in the world.

During his podcast, Bill said something that stuck with me. The interviewer asked him, "You've been an amazing influence on so many people in the marketplace. So how have you done that?" Bill answered that, as elementary as it may seem, in order to see God use people and to bring out the God-given gifts inside of them, you have to be "genuinely interested" in them and in what they want, and more interested in them than in your own church goals.

In answering that question, Hybels got to the core issue: actually loving people enough to walk with them.

I believe God wants us to be involved in the lives of people simply because businesses don't go to heaven or hell and products will not make it into the kingdom of God. I don't mean to imply that businesses, profits, and product development are not important. They are *incredibly* important, because they affect people's lives every day.

In order for us to have a genuine impact for the kingdom of God in the marketplace, we need to make course corrections in all things related to perspective. In the end, products aren't people and profit margins do not have a soul, but God wants to use you, as well as your products and your business models, to influence people.

It's people who matter. . .because people matter to God.

AN EXPERIENCE YET UNKNOWN

Heaven is going to be an experience like none other known to the human soul. There are many things about heaven that I look forward to. I anticipate that moment when I lock eyes with Jesus and hear His voice. And I anticipate meeting and talking with prophets like Amos.

What I think I anticipate most about heaven is that I will never again know what it is like to be a sinner.

THE DIFFERENCE IS NIGHT AND DAY

*If I say, "Surely the darkness will hide me and the light become
night around me," even the darkness will not be dark to you;
the night will shine like the day, for darkness is as light to you.*
PSALM 139:11–12

There are different kinds of dark. There's the dark you experience when you're in a major city and the ambient light doesn't allow you to see the night sky. There's the darkness that is half lit from security lights when you are trying to sleep in a hotel room. Then there's an all-consuming darkness, a darkness that wraps around you like a blanket, when you cannot see anything because you are in a remote area at night. No distant lights from a house a few miles away, no cell tower blinking on a ridge in the distance. It's hard to find that kind of darkness, but when you find yourself in it, you are consumed by it. There's an unmistakable vulnerability inside the heart when you're surrounded by that kind of darkness, regardless of how much of a man you think you are.

Maybe that's what David was getting at when he said that there are times when a situation seems so dark that it overwhelms the soul, the mind, and even the body. Yet David knew something about the Creator, an ambient truth with just enough glow to bring hope to the eyes of the heart: darkness never overwhelms God, for He created it. Darkness doesn't hide His glory, nor does it squelch His glorious ability to illuminate a path so we can follow Him even in the darkest of nights.

Darkness isn't dark to God at all, and no light is brighter to Him than the darkness is dark. They are one and the same to Him. You can trust that what is true about God's grace,

God's mercy, and God's sovereign ability to provide for you, regardless of the situation, is just as true in the dark as it is in the light. . .for His ability to see clearly is not bound to the process of illumination.

RELIEVED BY INABILITY

A few weeks back I was walking through an airport and saw a sign that bore this quote:

Everybody is a genius. But if you judge a fish by its ability to climb a tree, it will live its whole life believing that it is stupid.

—ALBERT EINSTEIN

All I could say was *amen*.

For the first several years of my ministry, I operated under the illusion that a leader must be well rounded—as in, I needed to be good at everything related to ministry. I've since learned that such an approach to life and career is not only toxically stressful, but not even biblical. You see, God never intended for any of us to be good at everything.

God made you with a specific gift mix, a specific mentality, and a specific personality so that you can maximize the "you" He intended you to be. Act outside of that, and you actually frustrate the very reasons He created you.

Many men who are obsessed with fear of failure see only their shortcomings. They become like Einstein's fish, which would spend its well-gifted life in the rut of depression because it focused on what it couldn't do—but was never intended to do in the first place.

The path to discovering why God created you begins with asking Him to reveal your calling and then measuring yourself only by your obedience to that calling, not by the distraction of that which He never called you to.

OBEDIENCE: IT'S NOT RELATIVE

I recently read an article that gauged reaction to the NAACP's endorsement of a presidential decision to support gay marriage. The article quoted many pastors on their thoughts about current efforts to bring this issue to the forefront of national conversation. I was amazed to read that several pastors admitted to having a hard time deciding exactly where to come down on that issue.

We are told in the media, almost daily, that if we do not support an individual's right to choose an "alternative lifestyle," then we are homophobic, uneducated, anti-intellectual, and hateful.

For a follower of Christ, however, the issue is this: either you believe the scriptures, or you don't. Either you accept God's sovereign rule over that which He created, or you don't. Obedience isn't relative. You don't get to pick and choose the areas in which you'll be obedient and still call yourself a devoted follower of Christ.

Yes, we all fail. We all sin. At times we all knowingly disobey our Lord, but that's not the defining point concerning obedience. A heart that is fully devoted to Christ is a heart that is resolved to do one's best to be obedient and to accept His truths as sovereign over all areas of life.

Pop culture will never have the biblical right to define obedience in the eyes of God. For a believer in Christ, the issues surrounding homosexuality actually aren't complicated at all. Let us not be deceived. Being filled with hatred is what makes you hateful. Obedience to God has nothing to do with hatred, and absolute resolve to honor God's Word doesn't make you a bigot but an unapologetic follower of the Lord God Almighty, who, in the end, is going to be your Judge.

Better to be a man who seeks to stand clean at the judgment than one who seeks to avoid the judgment of a culture that doesn't even try to understand what it means to be obedient to God.

LIFE: SUFFOCATED

Jesus calls us on a journey that is really something of an odyssey—a path of twists and turns in which He saves us from ourselves by withholding information about our earthly future, yet all the while giving us full disclosure about our eternal destination.

It's almost comical how we, each in our own way, covet knowing how the next chapter in our lives ends before it's even revealed. In truth, if God granted us that desire, it would stifle the growth that comes only as we learn to fully depend on Him and to trust His great love for those Christ has ransomed by His own blood.

Attempting to control life's unknowns only suffocates the very breath out of the experiences life gives. Life in Christ was never meant to be mechanical. This earthly journey consists of but two constants: there will always be changes in the landscape, and there will forever be a Guide for those who call upon His name.

SHARING WHAT YOU HAVE

How, then, can they call on the one they have not believed in? And
how can they believe in the one of whom they have not heard?
And how can they hear without someone preaching to them?

ROMANS 10:14

I recently ate lunch at a golf course. From my table, I could see a man on the driving range hitting ball after ball after ball. He was struggling—some of his shots were on line, but most of them were strays.

I grew up in the game of golf. My dad is a retired PGA professional. I've probably had more golf lessons than ten people who play the game, and that has taught me a lot about the fundamentals of the swing. Getting that knowledge from your head to your body is the tough part, which is why you don't see me playing on television on Sunday.

As I watched my fellow linkster beat range balls into submission, it occurred to me that no amount of time on the range was going to noticeably improve his game. He might improve a few strokes over time, but his golf game was fatally flawed for one reason: he simply didn't know how to improve it. His game and its future were forever hobbled by his lack of knowledge about the fundamentals.

This fellow on the range had it within him to be a solid golfer, if only he could come into the knowledge of how the swing actually works. He needed someone to teach him how to cure his reverse weight shift, how to improve his grip, and how to stop laying his club off so drastically at the top. He needed someone to tell him the truth, and if that were to happen, then he'd save a ton of money on equipment, his scores would be consistently lower, and he would actually enjoy golf more.

My guess is that if I had walked out to the range and started working with this guy in the orange shirt, then his game would have gotten better. That's not because I'm a great teacher of the game; it's just that I've been in his shoes. As the years have passed, I've learned more than he seemed to know about the fundamentals of the game. I'd be willing to bet that if I had approached him in the right spirit, taken some time to get to know him, and let him know I wasn't a "range pro" on an ego feed but was seeking to help him improve for his sake alone, then he would have welcomed my intervention.

You're going to encounter people who are spending a lot of time, energy, and money trying to figure out how to be happy. You're going to lock eyes with people who are grinding it out every day, hoping to catch a break and see changes for the better in their jobs, their marriages, or their finances. The sad reality is that they won't find happiness or fulfillment simply because there is no one to intervene and tell them the truth about life and what it means to know the Truth Giver who can set them free.

We often assume that nobody wants to hear what we have to say about our God. Think about this: When things were at their worst for you, when you knew you had lost your "swing" in life, were you looking for truth that could set you free? You bet you were! Don't let the enemy deceive you into thinking the people you encounter are not in search of a fresh breath of life and deliverance from their soul burdens.

WHO IS MY NEIGHBOR?

"Love your neighbor as yourself."
MARK 12:31

Not long ago, a friend of mine was faced with a trouble-some situation. As we talked, he brought up a solid question, one I've sought the answer to many times: "What is the will of God for me in this situation?"

As we began to work through the mechanics that made his issue so difficult, we began to see that the real question was, "What does love demand?" When Jesus said, "Love your neighbor as yourself," He meant it. The problem, at least for me, is determining my neighbor's identity. Are my business associates my neighbors? What about my *actual* neighbor Kevin and his family? Is someone in India I've never met my neighbor?

Today's world offers us many opportunities to intervene in the lives of people in need, but that doesn't mean you should respond to every need you see. Even Jesus didn't do that.

I am fully convinced that Jesus does not hold me responsible for everyone in the world. I believe He only holds me responsible for those God puts in my path. My neighbor Kevin is in my path, and so are my business colleagues. Occasionally—such as when my friend stoked this question once again in my heart—God puts someone in my path I cannot overlook or step over as if they are not there. I know they are there, and I am forced to deal with it, for God has put them there.

I must walk *to* them. . .because love demands it.

THIS SON OF MINE

For God so loved the world. . .
JOHN 3:16

I cannot help but think of what was running through his mind as the dust kicked up with each step. No doubt that dry dirt road was soaked with memories of throwing rocks, playing army, and building forts. He'd run down that road hundreds of times after hearing his mama calling him in for supper. He knew every rut, every bend, and every tree lining the ditches. But as he walked that same road this day, there was no mama calling him home, no father's voice filling the air—no sound from anyone, for nobody was expecting him. It had been too long. Perhaps they had stopped looking for him.

In the story of the prodigal son in Luke 15, Jesus tells us that the wayward son's dad saw him from a distance. I wonder what ran though the mind of this heartbroken father. I have two sons of my own; it's hard to imagine how I'd feel at the sight of one of them, the one whose heart had left the family, walking up the same road that had taken him toward his shame.

I have an idea, though, for this father revealed his heart toward the boy when he said, "This son of mine was dead and is alive again" (15:24).

"This son of mine." You see, this was personal to the dad. It's always personal when a father loses his son. The loss he feels is one only the deepest love can know. The pain is a type of pain only a father can feel. The boy didn't know it, but the day he walked out, he took his father's heart with him.

We tend to forget just how personal it is to the Father when any of His created ones leave home for a shameful land.

We call them "heathen," and they act the part well. We call them "lost" because they have chosen not to be found. We say such things because we tend to forget that there was a time when we, too, were on the other side of the cross, a time when we walked down the same road ourselves.

Never forget how the Father's heart aches when one of His treasures is lost because he chooses to travel to a land never intended for him. When one of His most prized possessions takes up residence in that barren land, it's personal, and He'll go to extreme measures to get him back.

OFFERING TITLED PROPERTY

*Do not offer any part of yourself to sin as an instrument
of wickedness, but rather offer yourselves to God as
those who have been brought from death to life.*

ROMANS 6:13

Imagine you're in church, and the sermon is over. The pastor calls for the ushers to come forward and take up the offering. When the bucket finally makes it to your row, you reach into your pocket and pull out a paper clip and place it in the bucket, along with a few pork rinds. After a little more searching, you find a used ink pen you got from the office (which was almost out of ink anyway) and put it in with the rest of your "offering."

Two factors are at play here: one is that you gave an offering that was worth absolutely nothing to you because it cost you nothing to give it. Second, and most striking, is that the offering is absurdly out of place.

The scriptures speak of the same irregularity in the life of a Christ follower who willingly gives himself as an offering. . .to sin.

When a person is without Christ, he's trying to live life under the power of his own authority, and that drives his every move. The ways in which he chooses to sin—whether it's sex outside of marriage or greed that motivates him to strive for a prize he doesn't even need—are irrelevant. A person demanding his own freedom from God's power will get just that—God's power—and the imminent danger that comes with it.

It's completely different with a Jesus follower. At least it should be.

When a believer in Christ willfully sins, he violates the basic nature of what it means to be renewed and transformed by the power of His resurrection. As a blessed American, you'd never dream of offering something as worthless as a stale pork rind to Holy God as your act of worship. It wouldn't be worthy of Him, and it bears no reflection of what He has done to secure your eternal salvation. It would show complete disregard for the power He has given you to navigate life in the fullness of the Spirit.

When Paul speaks of no longer offering yourself to sin, he's speaking of the simple fact that you are no longer obligated to obey an unredeemed sin nature. So don't give yourself as an offering to sin. Christ purchased your life and ransomed you from the dead. Therefore, never offer the devil property for which he has no deed or title.

ACCURATE ASSESSMENTS

"Watch out for false prophets. They come to you in sheep's clothing, but inwardly they are ferocious wolves. By their fruit you will recognize them. Do people pick grapes from thornbushes, or figs from thistles? Likewise, every good tree bears good fruit, but a bad tree bears bad fruit. A good tree cannot bear bad fruit, and a bad tree cannot bear good fruit. Every tree that does not bear good fruit is cut down and thrown into the fire. Thus, by their fruit you will recognize them."
MATTHEW 7:15–20

As a follower of Jesus, you can count on the devil to throw lots of distortion your way. Our enemy loves nothing more than to twist the scriptures to confuse the mind—and he's very good at it. He has managed to twist Jesus' words "Don't judge" to mean that Christians should never make assessments about the behavior and words of others. It seems that everywhere I go, I hear people—many of them followers of Christ—saying, "Well, it's not my place to judge."

But nothing could be further from the truth. The scriptures do, in fact, give you the right to judge righteousness from unrighteousness. Jesus told us plainly that "you'll know a tree by its fruit."

Where we go wrong is failing to draw a scriptural line between being judgmental and making wise judgment. The scriptures do not give us the right to be judgmental, which happens when we make character assessments about a person without knowing his situation or backstory.

The older I get, the more I realize that I must be slow, *very* slow, to form an opinion or conclusion about a person or situation until I know the facts. Only when I do that can I make the righteous assessments God calls His followers to make.

Even still, be careful not to make ill-informed assumptions, for they can lead you to a whopping lot of crow eating.

TELL THE TRUTH— TRUST GOD WITH THE OUTCOME

Do not lie to each other, since you have taken off your old self with its practices and have put on the new self, which is being renewed in knowledge in the image of its Creator.
COLOSSIANS 3:9-10

I used to work with a guy who had a tendency to lie at times. He wasn't what we'd think of as a habitual liar, but on occasions when a situation looked like it might reflect badly on him, he'd twist the truth or the circumstances so that the spotlight would be anywhere but on him.

I don't think this man was a bad person; in fact, I liked him and considered him a friend. He loved God and his family, and he was fun to be around. I don't believe that he ever got up in the morning intending to lie that day. However, when he was pressured, he'd panic—and in that panic, he'd say just about anything to disarm the stress. If that meant lying, then he'd do it, and then face the consequences later if anyone found out about his untruths.

When you lie, you reveal that you do not trust God with the outcome in a given situation. My friend simply could not help but try to manipulate situations in his favor, and if it meant burning a friend by speaking dishonestly, then he'd do it. In the end, it cost him relationships. His life, by his own admission, was built entirely upon fear that he'd fail, and sadly, the lying only brought him more failure. It was a self-imposed prison.

Charles Spurgeon once said, "Avoid cowardice, for it makes men liars."

When you are backed into a corner, tell the truth—*no matter what*. God is certainly bigger than your corner.

POLITICS AND RELIGION

We often hear the popular refrain that politics and religion should never mix. That line of thinking has been deeply ingrained into our popular culture's thinking, but it doesn't line up with what the scriptures teach. For example, nearly all of the Old Testament prophets stood toe to toe with the king ruling the land at the time to confront him about social injustices, immorality, and blatant disregard for God's principles.

Try telling the World War II–era German preacher Dietrich Bonhoeffer that politics and religion should never mix. You'd first have to exhume his body and bring it back to life to say it, for he died at the hand of the Nazis for opposing Hitler's regime.

Try telling the same thing to Youcef Nadarkhani, the pastor who spent long periods of time in an Iranian dungeon because he refused to give in when he was threatened with death if he didn't renounce his Christian faith and convert to Islam.

Many men and women of faith have risked everything to stand up for what they believe in. Yet too many Christians either don't speak out according to what they know the Word of God says, or don't bother to get involved by voting.

I know that I'll be judged one day according to how faithful I was to the Lord Jesus Christ and His mandates for life. If that loses me favor with my political party, then so be it. If it causes me to be called "radical," then that's just the way it is. If it causes some to unsubscribe from my writing because it's overtly political on occasion, then I'm okay with that. I'm committed to carrying the name of Jesus, no matter the cost, and that means I cannot support any nation, any government, or any candidate who openly works against everything the scriptures stand for.

It may make some of you uncomfortable to read this, but if you follow Jesus, then Jesus leads, period. And if you follow Jesus' lead, then you have an obligation to be His representative everywhere you go—including the voting booth. That means voting according to what you know God says is right, and not according to race, gender, or any other factor.

THE POWER OF ONE LIFE

If one part suffers, every part suffers with it.
1 CORINTHIANS 12:26

The sex-abuse scandal within the Penn State University Athletic Department, which broke into public view in 2011, is a tragic reminder to us all that one life matters and that one man's choices can have terrible effects on the lives of many people.

One life, and the choices of that one life, devastated dozens of families and damaged a university financially, academically, and athletically. Moreover, one man's sin affected his teammates and coaches and eventually led others to cover up his deeds. One man's terrible sin snowballed and plowed its way into the lives of others with relentless destruction.

A person would have to be a fool to think that one man's personal life is an island, secluded unto itself, that has no effect on others. The scriptures testify to the fact that we are in this thing called life together, with equal cause and effect. The Penn State scandal may be an extreme example, but it still serves as an illustration of the power of one man's sin to damage many other people.

Your life matters, and it matters to more than just yourself. As you live out your days, never forget that *everything* you do matters.

CAN GOD TRUST YOU?

"Whoever can be trusted with very little can also be trusted with much, and whoever is dishonest with very little will also be dishonest with much. So if you have not been trustworthy in handling worldly wealth, who will trust you with true riches? And if you have not been trustworthy with someone else's property, who will give you property of your own?"
LUKE 16:10–12

We often think of faith as placing our trust in God—and that is in fact a good definition of faith. Faith means trusting in "what is not seen." There is an area, however, where God looks to see if He can trust you: your money.

God is not offended at the idea of you making a profit. But He is offended when He pours out blessings on His children only to have them balk at His goodness by refusing to honor Him through tithing. We often pray for God to "bless" us with more. If we are not faithful with what we already have, then how can we expect Him to funnel more wealth our way? To do that would only lead to more unfaithfulness—and it is against God's nature to be a party to our sin.

God calls us to trust Him with the money He gives us. Do not be led to believe that He cannot provide for you if you're faithful to Him. In the end, every man is faced with a simple choice: Will he trust God enough to tithe out of obedience, or will he live in a lack of trust and hold with a tight grip the money God has given him? We are forced to make that choice, because we cannot "serve two masters."

A GREATER FORCE

*"These are the words of him who is holy and true,
who holds the key of David. What he opens no one
can shut, and what he shuts no one can open."*
REVELATION 3:7

Desire is an odd animal. It can drive you to achieve things that leave others in awe and wondering how you did it. Yet you know full well how you did it—through desire and hard work. Put those two together, and you're able to do things many others cannot.

But when you don't allow the Holy Spirit to be the master over your desire, it can serve as a fast track to the confinement of a self-constructed prison.

Never forget that no man can do for you what God can. What may take you a long career to even attempt, God can do for you in the blink of an eye. Changing unfathomable situations is as easy to Him as breathing is to you.

The beautiful thing about being in Christ is that you are no longer held hostage to the sway of any influence—including that of your own desires. No mortal can define your destiny or destroy your path, no matter how bleak things look through the temporary lens of this world. No competitor can outpace you, for while others pursue temporary gain, you strive for eternal rewards.

For those of us in Christ, the playing field is not equal. We are not playing by the same rules because we have chosen to submit to a supreme Ruler. When He opens doors for you, no power on earth can shut them. On such a playing field, you have no equal, and thus you have no need to force your will or your desires, simply because His will is greater for you on every front.

THE RIGHT STUFF

But mark this: There will be terrible times in the last days. People will be lovers of themselves, lovers of money, boastful, proud, abusive, disobedient to their parents, ungrateful, unholy, without love, unforgiving, slanderous, without self-control, brutal, not lovers of the good, treacherous, rash, conceited, lovers of pleasure rather than lovers of God—having a form of godliness but denying its power. Have nothing to do with such people.

2 Timothy 3:1–5

We often think of sin as loving all the wrong things, and it is most certainly that. When a man gives himself full license to sin and embraces his own path, the end result is that he will love all the wrong things.

Look at how the above scripture verse describes sinners: "lovers of themselves, lovers of money," "not lovers of the good," "lovers of pleasure rather than lovers of God," and so forth.

Your desire to love wasn't created in a vacuum. God created you to love, and He created you to aim that love at one target—Him. Satan is a deceiver, and he takes that inborn need to love and attempts to shift it toward anything and everything but God.

Think about it: you are made in God's image, and every emotion and every desire you have comes from Him. If you look closely behind the curtain of your heart, you may see how the enemy has polluted your emotions and desires, thus changing your wants and needs.

God created the desire for sex, but Satan has polluted that desire and turned it into lust. God founded your desire for security, including a security in knowing you will be with Him eternally, but Satan has polluted that, too, and made it into greed and a sinful desire for power.

Sin, however, isn't just about love for the wrong things. It's also about not loving the things worth loving, and that's what is at the heart of having a "form of godliness" that is devoid of power.

Satan can fill your appetites, but he can never satisfy the longing of your soul. Only God can do that. The difference is that God does it by giving you the things worth loving—including Himself.

BE ALARMED

Ever notice how many things we so closely guard in every-day life? We have smoke alarms to guard against being caught in a fire, car alarms to keep people from stealing our vehicles, alarms on our phone to let us know that we are about to miss an appointment or important phone call. We even have identity theft alarms to let us know if someone is trying to break into our bank account.

Alarms are a necessity of life, and for the most part they do a great job at guarding our stuff.

We spend a lot of energy and money guarding and protecting our stuff out of fear that dishonest people will take it away from us. The irony is that Jesus told us that the thing we should fear the most is not people who can steal from us or do us harm. He instructed us, "Do not be afraid of those who kill the body but cannot kill the soul. Rather, be afraid of the One who can destroy both soul and body in hell" (Matthew 10:28).

There's nothing wrong with taking steps to protect our physical bodies or the things we own. The Word of God, however, tells us that it's far more important to guard our hearts from the corruption of chasing things that do not matter in the end.

THE SECRET DRUMBEAT

"Do you have eyes but fail to see, and ears but fail to hear?"
MARK 8:18

Our younger son, Tucker, has on many levels pushed us farther down the road of faith in all things related to parenting. It seems like our first son, Cole, actually set Michelle and me up for parental failure by being too "good." From day one, Cole was compliant, gentle, reliable, and just about as easy to raise as a child could be. But Tucker? Well, he simply isn't any of that. Not yet, anyway.

Tucker is incredibly funny, but compliant he is not. Since the day Tucker was born, it was obvious that at the top of his core value system was total defiance of authority. Gentle? Yes, sometimes. Reliable? Very much so, at least in terms that you can absolutely count on him. . .to destroy just about anything you find valuable. Tucker has redefined the concept of man-to-man defense for me—as in, I have to shadow him at every moment to keep him from scoring.

I'll give Tucker this: he is a winner. He will find a way to score, and the prize is always at the peril of my bank account. Bookies in Vegas could win big-time if they laid down odds that he will surpass the number of spankings Cole received by the age of seven before he's three years old.

In all fairness to Tuck, he's a ton of fun—at least when he's not drawing a line in the sand for control of whatever is important to him at the moment. One of the things Tucker has taught me is that there's always a party going on. . .as long as you have the desire to find it.

Before Tucker could even walk, we'd notice him bobbing his head at times—like he was at a rock concert in the arena of his head. Whether we were at a grocery store or walking through a parking lot—in a noise-filled environment of any sort—out of nowhere, Tuck would start moving to a groove. Yet when we listened closely, we'd hear the beat somewhere in the background—sometimes soft, sometimes loud, but always there.

I am fully convinced that Tucker is going to teach me a lot about God—especially about the joy in the heart of a heavenly Father who yearns for His children to enjoy the journey set before them. His song is always playing during that journey, if we have "eyes to see and ears to hear."

IMAGINE THE SURPRISE

When a Samaritan woman came to draw water. . .
JOHN 4:7

The irony of it all is that He wasn't supposed to be there. Not by her thinking anyway.

When the woman went to the well (see John 4), she went during the middle of the day. Women were often the ones who retrieved water for their homes, and they did so in the early morning or late evening—but never in midday. The woman's intent was to slip in and slip out quickly, without being seen.

I can't help but imagine her expression and what went through her mind as she walked up to the well and found someone sitting there.

"Are you kidding me? . . . Seriously?"

This woman had some serious sins in her past: she didn't mind sleeping with men. She was an outcast in a society of people who were already seen as outcasts, so you might say she was an accomplished sinner. (I suppose even outcasts need someone to pick on for the sake of spiritual self-esteem.)

Imagine her shock when Jesus told her not only that she'd had five husbands, but also that He knew she wasn't married to the guy she was sleeping with at the time.

She was spot on to be shocked by the situation, because Jesus, the Son of God, was sitting there waiting on her.

We all have "wells" we've either visited or are now visiting. . .full of guilt and shame. My experiences with people—at their less-than-fine moments—is that most of the time, their wells are not so much gross and horrible as they are just flat-out embarrassing.

The sad reality is that we believe that the rest of the world would react with shock and awe. . .if they only knew about our private journeys to those caverns of water that didn't turn out quite as we'd hoped when we clutched that dipper.

That's the comedy in all of this for me: Jesus already knew the woman at the well had issues.

That was her "well," and she was being forced to face it head-on.

Each of our wells is unique. For some men, your well is greed and the private guilt you feel over wanting more stuff. For others, it is the frustration you feel because you know that women turn your head all the time, and you hate the fact that short skirts can send you to a mental abyss that has the potential to wreck your entire day. For some men it's living with constant battles over self-worth, and that's just something you believe a "real man" should never battle. For some, it is wanting to leave your wife and the shame that comes with feeling that way, because after all, a real Christian would never feel that way.

Yes, our wells may be different, but we all have them.

The more quickly we realize that every man has his own well full of embarrassments, the faster we then can get on with living in the freedom that comes from the Life Giver, who sits by our well, waiting on the conversation we've so desperately tried to avoid.

THE POWER OF YOUR CALL

Hang around preachers enough, and you're sure to hear the word *calling* come up. Most every preacher you meet has his own story of how God called him into the ministry. I wonder, however, if other believers ever think about God calling them to, well. . .anything at all.

While I know for certain that my call from God to full-time ministry was real and tangible, I am fully convinced that God doesn't just reserve the calling to the prophetic fraternity. Why? Because Moses was an average guy, David was a shepherd, and Amos was a fig farmer.

The scriptures say that you are "fearfully and wonderfully made" (Psalm 139:14). God took time to make you, and He doesn't waste His energy creating a worthless product.

Every one of us is called to something. Calling is not a guarantee of success or of failure. Calling is not exclusive to any group, like, say, pastors. Your calling is, however, unique to you. Most importantly, calling is about obedience, not the task ahead.

Following your calling comes down to courage and guts. Do you have the fortitude to stay on a path when it gets hard or to go where God tells you to go even though life is comfortable?

My calling has been, and always will be, the only constant I can truly depend on in terms of my career and my identity. My identity is shaped by the fact that God told me He wanted me walking a certain path. You have the same kind of calling. The context of your career may not be the same as mine, but your decision to be obedient to His call on your life is what's at stake.

Never be afraid to walk into the unknown when God has called you to do it. It's there and only there that you'll find a freedom that transcends circumstance.

A CALL TO ACTION

So much has been said about the last presidential election. Never in my lifetime have I seen my country so polarized about the direction we will take for our future.

It has occurred to me, however, that no matter what our country decides in an election, our moral and spiritual compass will remain pointed in a direction other than true north. I believe our country has been slipping steadily away from God for a long, long time, and we should never be duped into thinking that one election can change our current path.

America desperately needs vocal, passionate, unyielding men of God who have true grit. We need prophets who will speak His truth, prophets who will warn people of God's coming judgment. And I believe that the Holy Spirit is now summoning valiant warriors to proclaim the way of the Lord.

No election will change the fact that America badly needs men of God who are willing to work to permeate their personal spheres of influence with His presence. Never before has so much hung in the balance.

THE PARABLE OF THE DITCH

There's an old cliché about driving that you may have heard before: "Keep it between the ditches." Sounds easy enough, but as the journey of life moves forward at full throttle, you can easily find yourself headed straight for the ditch. Life is a constant expedition in real-time course correction.

Jesus spoke into our journey of manhood when He said, "Can the blind lead the blind? Will they not both fall into a pit?" (Luke 6:39).

No man can escape this simple truth: we are all under some influence. The question we all need to ask ourselves is, "What, or who, is doing the influencing?"

No man has ever been able to escape the powers and forces of his relationships. We are all tied at the heart to the influence of those we let into our lane of travel. And even though you know Jesus is your ultimate Guide, do not be so naive to think that He's the only one influencing you. It is quite easy to piously reject the notion that you are vulnerable to being swayed.

You have people traveling with you. Some you have invited on this journey, and others are there by simple sovereign connection in the marketplace of commerce and community. It doesn't really matter how they got there, for they are in the thick of it with you now. Watch and be sure that you are not being guided by those who are themselves blinded to the truths of Christ.

RUN TO FINISH

"However, I consider my life worth nothing to me; my only aim is to finish the race and complete the task the Lord Jesus has given me—the task of testifying to the good news of God's grace."
ACTS 20:24

The goal of starting any race is to finish. Anyone can start a race. In fact, millions start, but only a very small percentage actually finish.

No race worth running is without the unexpected. The great thing about living for Jesus is that a trip or a fall doesn't have to be a failure. If you offer the stumbles to Him as acts of worship and learning, they will become trophies of His grace and glory in you as you continue to run.

Christ in you is the hope of glory, say the scriptures. So stay in the race!

Though you may have scars, and though your stride may be forever altered, remember that no warrior comes home from a battlefield without scars—scars that may not even be visible to others.

So run your race, but run it to finish. For it is in running that you will eventually cross the finish line and earn victory and see His glory.

AN INNER FILTER

*The person with the Spirit makes
judgments about all things.*
1 CORINTHIANS 2:15

At that supernatural moment when you came into the family of God through a personal relationship with Christ, a cosmic amount of God's heart was downloaded into your life. Not only were you redeemed, but you immediately received the assets of redemption. One such asset was an inner filter for truth.

The Holy Spirit is your Guide, your filter for truth. As Jesus told His disciples, "But when he, the Spirit of truth, comes, he will guide you into all the truth" (John 16:13).

Lies, heresy, and deception come in many forms. The older I get, the more I see how eternally valuable my filter for truth is in all matters pertaining to the journey of manhood.

God gave you a filter, so use it. If you don't, you'll find out quickly—*very* quickly—that an unfiltered life is cluttered with every imaginable impurity.

BLESSED RECONCILIATION

All this is from God, who reconciled us to himself
through Christ and gave us the ministry of reconciliation.
2 CORINTHIANS 5:18

One of the toughest days of my life took place during an elk hunt. My cameraman and I had just finished eating lunch when the outfitter gently told me, "Jason, you need to call home. We received a ham radio message that your wife is trying to contact you."

Some dear friends from the outfitter's camp handed me a satellite phone and told me, "Don't worry about the minutes." Perched at eleven thousand feet on that mountain, I called my wife's cell number. All I could do was look down and brace myself, for I knew it couldn't be good. In my mind's eye, I can still see my Danner boots, worn from trekking the Rockies of northern New Mexico.

Michelle answered, and the conversation went exactly like this:

Michelle: *Hello.*

Me: *Hey, it's me. I'm on a satellite phone. The reception is not great. Is everything okay?*

Michelle: *Honey, I'm so sorry. Dat died.*

That was it. The call dropped and the phone went silent.

My grandfather, Josh "Dat" Cruise, had suffered from chronic heart problems for many years. I knew I'd get this call one day, but I had no idea it would come when I was days from home in the mountains.

I got in my truck and drove hours out of the mountains to the first small town I could find, hoping to locate a pay phone. Once I reached a phone, I called my dad, who told me that Dat had left for his eternal reward two days before I found out. In the previous two days, my family had tried to call me, but I was in the mountains and couldn't be reached.

This all meant there was no way I could make it to Dat's funeral, which was scheduled for the next day. Still I wanted to try, but Dad insisted that I hunt, even though we both knew I didn't want to be there.

I did what my daddy told me to do. I finished out the hunt, but my mind was on losing my grandfather. I felt robbed of Dat's presence, and that was a foreign feeling, for he'd always been there for me. He was at all of my ball games, and he was there the first time I shot a gun. He was there for all of our trips to the cabin, where he, my daddy, and all his buddies would chase whitetails. Now he was gone.

The only thing that kept me from losing my mind was that Dat and I were not estranged. We were together in our hearts. Our relationship was wonderful and solid. In fact, it had always been that way. We were one in heart and in mind. There were no lost chapters in our past left unrecovered, no bad words left unredeemed. He loved me, and I loved him. We not only loved one another but had spoken our love frequently so that there would be no assuming it.

In that moment I finally understood the gravity of love and harmony in life, for all things become clear when you get a phone call that drives you to your knees. It's hard for me to imagine a pain more intense than what I felt on that New Mexico elk hunt. I suppose the only way it could have been worse was if there had been lost chapters unrecoverable and bitter words unredeemed.

There is no other time in your life when you are most like Jesus than when you forgive a trespass. There is no other time in your life when you share His love more than when you reconcile with those from whom you have been estranged. My prayer for you today is that you accept the call to the "ministry of reconciliation."

Dat's birthday is November 28.

I miss my granddad.

RUNNING DOWN A DREAM

My son, pay attention to my wisdom, turn your ear to my words
of insight, that you may maintain discretion and your lips may
preserve knowledge. For the lips of the adulterous woman
drip honey, and her speech is smoother than oil; but in the
end she is bitter as gall, sharp as a double-edged sword. . . .
For your ways are in full view of the LORD, and he examines
all your paths. The evil deeds of the wicked ensnare them;
the cords of their sins hold them fast. For lack of discipline
they will die, led astray by their own great folly.
PROVERBS 5:1–4, 21–23

Every fall, avid deer hunters live their annual dream—chase big bucks, go to work, be a husband and father, all while trying to survive for about sixty days of total sleep deprivation.

Several seasons back, a friend of mine invited me to hunt a farm near his home in the Midwest. I was honored, for I'd always wanted a chance to chase the big whitetails in that region. In fairy-tale fashion, I arrowed what has been my largest buck to date: a fourteen-pointer with a double main beam that scored just shy of 160 inches. The hunt itself was absolutely amazing.

The chase phase of the rut was in full swing, so I was committed to an all-day sit. At 3:00 p.m., however, I climbed down from the oak to go and sit on the ground about 110 yards north of my stand site. It seemed like a good place to sit because all day long I'd noticed deer crossing the intersection of a wood line and a field edge. It was a horribly risky move because there wasn't a lot of cover for a ground assault. I knew I was out of position, so I had to do something.

One hour later, with the temperature dropping, this brute hopped a fence and came into the cut bean field about four hundred yards from my position under a cedar tree. With his nose glued to the ground on a trot, he began working my way. He was locked onto a hot doe's scent trail. When he was ninety yards away I grunted at him, and he swung his monster head in my direction. I grunted a second time, and he grunted back and then began to sprint directly at me, running down what he felt was an opportunity to satisfy his greatest craving. He closed the gap from ninety yards to twelve yards in roughly six seconds. On one knee crouched in sage grass, I shot him at twelve paces. To use a worn-out cliché, it was truly the "hunt of a lifetime."

The most elusive animal in North America is a large whitetail buck. No animal is better at staying alive, and no animal is better at adaptation to a hostile environment, than a whitetail buck. Yet this elusive, wise, savvy survivalist was shot and killed for one simple reason: he was temporarily living off the adrenaline of pure emotion.

SCRIPTURE INDEX

ABOUT THE AUTHOR

Jason Cruise is a nationally known speaker, published author in the world of men's ministry, and host of *Spring Chronicles* on the Sportsman Channel. His fingerprints are on many of the resources in publication today that engage outdoorsmen to discover strategies that connect a love for hunting with their love for God. He lives in Tennessee with his wife, Michelle, and their two boys, Cole and Tucker.

www.JasonCruise.com
Twitter: @JasonLCruise
Facebook: Facebook.com/JasonLCruise